Divine
Renovations

A Carpenter, His Soul Mate and Their Story of Love and Loss

Janice Beetle

Off the Common Books
Amherst, MA | 2013

Off the Common Books, Amherst, MA

Cover design by Lisa Stowe

Edited by Margot Cleary

ISBN: 978-1-4675-6810-4

Family and Relationships. English. 2013. 173 pages.

For Ed

Prologue

When people learn that my husband, Ed Godleski, passed away, one of the first questions they ask is how long we were married. When I tell them two years, they say "Oh" in such a way that I know they think this can't hurt as much as losing the man you've been with your whole adult life. Sometimes I'm compelled to add that I was with Ed for eight years, three of which I lived with him. I know it doesn't change what they think, and then I remember that what they think doesn't matter.

What does matter is how much I miss Ed. It matters that it feels like I knew him forever. It feels like in losing him, I lost myself. Perhaps some people calculate grief by multiplying "number of years together" with "love we had." And that's why they don't understand my heartache because while the years we had were few, the love was incalculable.

Ed was my soul mate, my best friend, my lover and the person I wanted to spend the rest of my life with. He died September 14, 2010, in my arms, in our living room, four months after he was diagnosed with metastatic lung cancer. His death hit me in a place I can't name, and learning how to cope with my grief has been a surreal journey.

I'm an optimistic person, as well as hard-working and loving, but I became a shell of myself after Ed died. For months, I couldn't sleep or eat. I cried every day, sometimes all day, and I wandered around aimlessly, thinking I could find Ed somewhere, if I looked hard enough. I learned what it means to keen. I learned that when you sob, you begin to drool. Losing Ed aged me.

I learned that twilight was the hardest time of day. As the sun began to set, I realized that 24 more hours had passed without a single sighting of Ed. I realized, over and over again, that he was truly gone.

On one particularly bad day, only several weeks after Ed died, my 17-year-old daughter, Molly, was at work, and I was home alone in the early evening. Grief engulfed me. My chest was tight. I was sobbing, and before I knew it, I was in a fetal position on my living room floor, covered with the green down comforter my friend Judy gave to Ed to keep him warm.

I clutched the urn that held Ed's ashes, my face pressed against the rough mosaic surface. I carried on, calling his name, bemoaning the unfairness of it all, until I heard the car door slam. Molly was home. I returned the urn to the piano and myself to the couch.

My breakdown changed nothing. Ed did not come home. I did not feel happy. I did not get anything "out of my system." But this particular episode changed me in that it gave me an idea. I would write a book.

Grief — of all kinds — takes us to some awful places. It is profoundly altering, and I want others to know — perhaps those just arriving on this loneliest of journeys — that they are not the first ones here. They are not alone. And they will find a way, as I did, to fit back into the world.

Chapter One

It's hard to say when Ed Godleski became my Great Obsession, instead of just the carpenter who came to renovate the kitchen. I was 39 when I met him, the mother of two beautiful daughters, 9 and 13. I'd been married for 15 years.

The first time we spoke was Memorial Day in 2002. My family and I were driving home from New Hampshire, where we'd spent the weekend at my parents' house on Lake Winnisquam.

I was involved in car games with my daughters, singing songs and playing the alphabet game, using billboards and road signs and license plates to find As and Bs and Cs, racing to be the first to get all the way to Z.

"Hello?" I answered my cell phone, shushing the girls.

Ed introduced himself. "I'm the carpenter assigned to your renovation job, and I wondered if I might stop by tomorrow so you can sign the contract."

"Oh, sure," I said. "I'm so excited."

I'd waited for years to have the money to renovate the kitchen of our home on Beacon Street in Florence, Massachusetts. I knew exactly what I wanted done. We settled on 5 p.m. the next day, and I hung up with not another thought for this Ed person, this carpenter I did not know. I told my husband the carpenters would start soon. Neither one of us knew this moment would mark the beginning of the end of our marriage.

Ed's hands were what I noticed the next day when he came to the house, a yellow bungalow with unpainted wooden trim and an expansive front porch. Ed's right hand was planted on top of the contract, so it wouldn't move while I was signing, and it was just so large. It suggested strength and skill.

Ed and his partner, Tex, showed up on Wednesday, and I watched as they unloaded tools, surveyed the situation and began stripping off trim boards around the doorway that led to the dining room. I offered them tea, and I let them know they were welcome to use our refrigerator, our water faucet, our bathroom.

"People love to see us come," Ed told me, "But at the end of a job, they love to see us go even more."

I could imagine that ringing true for me. But I was wrong.

Ed first became a distraction one afternoon about a week after he and Tex arrived. I worked at home, running a writing, editing and graphic design business called Beetle Press, and I was also a stay-at-home mom for the girls. But during this particular moment, they were in school.

I was walking toward the kitchen, lost in thought. Tex was on a ladder in the middle of the kitchen when the basement door opened. The sound caused me to look up, and there was Ed, tall, muscular, a head full of thick gray hair, all of which I had not previously noticed. We locked eyes, and a palpable energy passed between us, like a physical experience of emotional intimacy. It was intense, but it was brief, and afterward, I wanted to shout, "Did you feel that? What the hell was it?"

We didn't speak, but I knew at that moment that Ed was in my house for some reason other than renovation. It seemed we had a spiritual connection. I believed that God was sending me a message.

I had believed in God and angels and spirits my whole life, but not because I had a religious upbringing. My parents were not churchgoers, yet I was a closeted believer. I didn't know why I believed in a life after death or angels in heaven until my mother told me that she went to the hereafter when she was giving birth to me. She didn't call it "the hereafter," though; she called it outer space.

My mother tells it this way: She went into labor with me on the same day that President John F. Kennedy was shot. She was admitted to Needham Hospital, and prepped for labor and delivery. After being anesthetized, she went to outer space, where she watched the lives of everyone she'd lost pass by her eyes.

"John Beetle," my mother said, speaking of my brother, who died at 10 of leukemia, before I was born. "As his name passed by, like it was on a screen, I knew his life was passing by, too."

"Then I saw my mother's name. Muriel Jefferson," she said. "It all just passed right by me. Once their name had passed over the top of my head, I knew that meant their life was over."

As she told the story, my mother held her hands several feet apart. That's how big the words were, she said, before they scrolled up and out of sight.

My mother listed the other names she'd seen. Her father's. Her brother Jackie's; he also died of leukemia, at 14.

"Where did you say you were, Mom?" I asked, hearing this story for the first time in my 30s. Something important had occurred to me.

"I was dreaming that I was in outer space. I was floating in outer space."

"No. It wasn't a dream, and you weren't in outer space," I said, "I think you had a near-death experience while you were in labor. You were in the hereafter, Mom."

She said when she came to, the anesthesiologist *did* ask her pointedly how she was feeling and seemed to express concern for her.

To me, that explained everything about who I was, who I'd become. I was a spiritual soul because my mother left this earth for a time while I was being born.

This story of my mother's is mine now, too, but we will each have to tell it in our own way because outer space is a more comfortable destination for my mother than Heaven. If she ever tells the story to anyone again, my mother will still say she was in outer space, but that's okay. It all makes sense to me.

Chapter Two

My friend Bonni says she knew I loved Ed from the first day he arrived. She says I blurted out, "The carpenter's cute" as we sat having our afternoon glass of wine.

"Janice!" she exclaimed.

"What?" I said. "He's just cute."

She gave me a look.

My husband, Bill, was a cradle Episcopalian with a strong faith in God. It was one of the things that had first attracted me to him. When I was young and trying to find my way spiritually, he was the conduit I needed to get to God.

I wasn't baptized as a child. After losing my brother Johnny, my parents stopped attending the local Congregational church, and talk about God in our house led into conversation on why they no longer felt church was important.

Their minister had handled very poorly the anticipation of my brother's death. Three weeks before Johnny died, he pulled up in front of their house in a station wagon packed to the gills for vacation. Wearing a Hawaiian shirt, he knocked on the door to tell my parents he was going out of town, and if they were to need the services of a minister before his return, to call his office, and someone would help them make a connection. When my mother began to cry, he said, "Don't worry. Death is a beautiful thing."

That interaction cooled my mother on attending church, so we didn't talk about God, or Johnny, because it was all just too painful for my parents.

I believed in God, though, and in bed at night, I would talk to Him, ask Him to keep my parents safe because I couldn't live without them. I believed in more than God. I believed in souls, and I believed that even inanimate objects had them. I was the girl who knelt in front of my mother's chartreuse Mustang convertible after my oldest brother Jeff totaled it in a car accident. I wept, saying, "I'm sorry my brother wrecked you."

After my husband and I were married in 1987, going to church on Sundays became a part of our lives, and I soon came to know the peace and comfort of belonging in a spiritual family. I listened as the lay Eucharistic ministers read the prayers of the people. I sang hymns with a passion I didn't know I possessed. I learned the Nicene Creed, and after I was baptized at 25, I learned how to receive Communion. I learned what a spiritual journey was and learned that I was on one.

Hearing the prayers of the people moved me to such a degree that I became a lay Eucharistic minister myself. Repeating the words, "The blood of Christ, the cup of Salvation," I silently connected with people as they knelt at the altar to drink from the chalice I held. I felt the pain of those I knew to be experiencing a crisis, like the middle-aged man whose son had committed suicide or those who seemed to have come to the Communion rail to relieve a longing that was palpable to me. I felt others' joy, too. I felt the Holy Spirit, and I began to pray in a more focused way.

Everlasting Lord, please watch over my parents and keep them safe. Watch over my daughters and give them strength and courage and good health as they grow into the people you want them to be.

My prayers were always about my parents or my children, or those who I knew needed healing. I never prayed for my husband or myself. A time would come, though, when many of my prayers would be for forgiveness, for myself, and healing, for him.

By 1993, my husband and I had our two girls, Sally and Molly, and we were all

involved at St. John's. I took turns caring for babies in the church nursery during services. As a family, we attended pancake suppers. We helped fellow parishioners move to new homes. We pledged money we did not have. I even spent two terms on the church's vestry, its governing body.

This new faith was something I'd been searching for since I was a child talking to God in my bed, singing along to a musical version of The Lord's Prayer on my "Hits of the '60s" album. This faith made it impossible for me to stop thinking about why God brought me Ed.

Here are the things I knew about myself when I met Ed: I loved my children, and I loved being a mother. I loved being part of the community and being a writer and a business owner. I loved my ever-expanding social circle.

But I also knew that down-deep, in a place I let no one see, I was angry, resentful, bitter. I accepted these feelings as traits that developed in adulthood. I didn't question their roots. My life lacked passion and emotional connection. I accepted that that was the way it was.

I was curious about the renovation process, and I interviewed Ed's boss and wrote a piece on our project for the local paper. I was equally curious about Ed. So I made excuses to talk with him. We talked about project add-ons: exposing the brick chimney in the dining room, adding a skylight to the new entryway, tucking a dishwasher next to the sink. My husband had always left the decorating to me. I liked this because it meant I was in control. I didn't know until I left the marriage that I had needed more discussion, more debate, more back and forth. I wish there had been less control.

I liked Ed's taste, his ideas about blending the old with the new, using a wooden door for the new back entry to our 1900s home instead of a steel door, for instance. I liked the way Ed paid attention to detail.

I also liked the way Ed shared his opinions with me. After the white kitchen cabinets were installed, I painted the walls an ivory color and tried my hand at skim coating in pale greens and blues. My husband thought it looked fine. I did not. Ed suggested that I try something different. The skim coating looked like abstract art on the wall – very busy. I painted the walls Montgomery White. Again, my husband thought it was fine, but it seemed bland to me. When I asked Ed for his opinion the next day, he said he thought there wasn't enough contrast between the walls and the cabinets. That night I painted the walls Concord Ivory, a deep yellow.

"There it is," Ed said when he came in the next day. "That's the color."

It was the color I liked best as well.

My husband loved his work as a financial advisor and had a passion for learning. I was focused on my home, obsessed even, with creating a magazine look, with making sure that the house was clean and tidy and bright. Our minds were never on the same thing at the same time, unless we were talking about our children or discussing a book or movie.

One night he came home from work in the midst of chaos: I had decided to paint the dining room, and had chosen a color that was nearly purple to cover the old Navajo White. You couldn't miss the eggplant color, the pungent smell of the paint or the fact that I was standing on a ladder instead of making dinner.

"How do you like it?" I asked him as he passed through the room, shaking off his trench coat, eyes on the floor.

"What?" he answered.

"The color!"

"The color of what?" he said, growing irritated.

"The paint!"

He said he liked it, but history told me he wasn't interested enough to care. I was desperate for a conversation about the contrast, the new look, the evolution of our house. He was desperate to sit down and read the paper.

My mornings during that summer of 2002 began with a cup of decaffeinated coffee and then a run with my friend Justine. We were training for a marathon in October, in Maine, raising money for the American Cancer Society to honor my brother Johnny and Justine's late father. After the runs, I showered and sipped another cup of decaf on the couch in the living room where it so happened I could glimpse Ed arriving in his truck. After he turned his truck off, he would sit and sip from a to-go tea cup. I had begun to offer tea to him and to Tex during the day, but they always preferred to drive to Cooper's Corner, the local convenience store. Ed paid me no attention whatsoever.

In the mornings, as he sat in his truck for five minutes, 10 minutes, I wondered what he was thinking about, and it was in watching him this way that I began to imagine him as unhappy. This was not at all a sign — to me or to my husband, with whom I discussed my observations — that I was overly focused on the carpenter. I was a rescuer then, believing I could help others in need. I invited people to stay with us if they were in transition. For weeks at a time, I took care of the daughter of a woman who suffered from bipolar disorder. In my own head, and in my husband's, Ed was simply my newest mission.

I was certain Ed was either divorced or widowed, that something haunted him, and I remember feeling betrayed when I learned he had a wife. I also felt jealous when Ed mentioned in passing, as he was leaving one night, that he was going out for a beer with his friend Kelly — until I learned that Kelly was a man.

But even this jealousy failed to signal that something was amiss. I did not, for one second, look inward at the reasons behind my growing obsession. I simply felt a calling, a pull. I had come to believe that Ed was like a soul mate, delivered to me by God. I needed to find out why, and the why, I was sure, was in something I could do for him, not in something he could do for me.

I had a new story about Ed for Bonni every day.

"I think he's my soul mate," I told her. "I think God sent him to me."

I believed this as deeply as I had once believed that Johnny was my guardian angel. I even confessed to having a crush on Ed.

"Are you worried?" Bonni asked.

"Worried about what?"

Even though I had many times admitted to Bonni that I felt angry and resentful toward my husband, I saw marriage as permanent. I grew up surrounded by angry couples who had stayed married. Ending a marriage, even thinking about it, did not remotely seem like a choice. Besides, I had had crushes before, and they always passed.

What I failed to understand then was that I had never — ever — had feelings for a man that had roots in emotional, as well as physical, attraction.

During the renovation, my mother came for a visit. We were fierce Scrabble competitors back then, and we played our games in the dining room as Ed worked outside, just on the other side of the window.

"That man has a beautiful head of hair," my mother said.

"I've noticed," I told her, smiling. "I have a wicked crush on him."

"Janice!" she scolded.

"What? Relax. It's just a crush. It's not like I'm going to run away with him."

Ed brought treats for the dog, our black Lab retriever mix, Angus. He brought his lunch in a small green cooler. He ate soup when it was 97 degrees and humid outside. He was a musician. He had three sons and sometimes brought home takeout Chinese for them. These things I knew from watching and listening out my second-floor window, my home office for Beetle Press.

Ed was sensitive and kind. He was a nurturer, like Bonni, like me. I knew this because he listened. One afternoon when I had no deadlines, I was in the kitchen, watching Ed work. He was on his hands and knees, removing the spacers between the ceramic tiles a mason had laid in the new back entryway. I started to help him. Ed told me his father was sick, that he had cancer. I wondered if this was the source of the unhappiness I sensed, and I tried to draw more from him.

Ed didn't want to talk about his father's illness, but he did begin to talk about his father, how he had been a respected teacher at Northampton High School, chair of the Math Department. His father had served in the Korean War and, during that time, Ed and his mother and sister lived with his mother's parents on their farm in Hatfield. He told me how his grandfather would cuss at the woodchucks who nibbled on each and every squash, how his grandfather would have gladly given them a bushel to eat in exchange for leaving the rest of the crop alone. I told Ed I spent my summers on Lake Winnisquam in a camp that was close to the railroad tracks. When I heard the whistle blow, I told him, I would run to the tracks and line pennies on the rail, then wait to gather them after the train had gone by. They were hot in my fingers.

A few days later, I walked out my new back door and noticed a short length of rail set like a sculpture in my garden. I walked over for a closer look and saw a penny resting on it. I asked everyone in my family, "Did you put that there?"

They did not.

One morning in July 2002, I woke up laughing. My husband was awake, leaning against the headboard.

I continued laughing, waiting for him to ask me what was so funny, rather than offering it up. I kept waiting. He didn't ask.

I couldn't stand it, so I said, "I had the funniest dream."

Again, I waited. He didn't ask me what the dream was about. It was this kind of disappointing interaction that had put loneliness and resentment in my heart.

In July that summer, my husband had a hip replacement. I remember being detached, almost apathetic, and visited him only two or three times in the hospital during his week-long stay.

When he came home, I got him settled in our room, made him lunch, and then I went downstairs and refinished the dining room table. It never occurred to me to play cards with Bill, keep him company. I did not give him enough.

By late August, Ed and Tex were almost done with our kitchen. They had expanded the opening into the dining room, sealed off an entrance that made no sense and created new cabinet and counter space. They had added an entryway and a downstairs bathroom and installed a brand-new dishwasher, a luxury I'd been without since we'd moved in.

The house, always beautiful but for the kitchen, was now truly gorgeous. I loved it. I loved to lie on the wicker chaise I'd put in the kitchen and stare up through the skylight that had been Ed's idea.

The thought that he would soon leave made me cry, incessantly. I told my husband one night, as we shared a bottle of Chardonnay, drinking more than we should have, as we did most every night, "I love Ed."

He said, "I know you do."

He thought I meant platonic love. I no longer knew.

Bonni and I spent most afternoons and evenings together, taking turns cooking for each other and helping each other with the children. We nurtured each other. We even called each other "Wife." Our friendship was part of the reason I did not know that I wasn't happily married. When I needed emotional contact, I had Bonni.

"You know what I want for my 15th wedding anniversary?" I asked her one evening as we sipped wine on her deck.

"No, what?" she wondered.

"A weekend with Ed."

She asked me if I was worried yet, and I said, "No."

"What are you going to do?" my friends asked me at a girl's night out at Bonni's when I talked about how much I was going to miss the carpenter.

"Nothing," I said. "What can I do? I would never leave my husband."

I meant this. I had no thoughts about leaving, no daydreams about it during the day, no fantasies late at night. Divorce would upend the picture-perfect marriage I had duped the world — and myself — into believing I had.

On Ed's last day of work at the Beacon Street house, I gave him a ceramic sculpture of a house and a card in which I had copied what I thought was a friendship poem. I'd found it in a book of poems the cashier at Cooper's Corner had loaned to me. If you'd asked me that day to name the feelings behind the gesture, I would have labeled them "compassion," "kindness." And on the day I copied that poem into a greeting card and tucked it in an envelope with Ed's name on it and left it on the passenger seat of his pick-up, I would have described the nature of the relationship I wanted to have with him as "friend."

But in bed that night, I read and re-read that poem. The stanzas that seemed so innocent when I copied them in the card — with words that spoke of bees and summer and flowering fields — had a not-really-so-subtle message that I had over-looked. It hinted of passion and solitude between lovers.

Reading the words made my heart race. What had I been thinking? What had I done? What would Ed do? Would he respond? I was terrified, and when Ed called two days later to ask if he could come back to Beacon Street to take photographs for his work portfolio, he didn't mention my note, but he did mention he had a gift for me. I hoped that we could begin to carve out a relationship much like the one I had with Bonni. While I considered Ed a good-looking man, it was largely the emotional piece that drew me to him.

Ed brought CDs of his favorite artists, Kasey Chambers and Norah Jones among them, as well as some of his own music. He was a songwriter and a bass player. Ed also brought me a necklace — silver with blue, inlaid gemstones — and I put it on. I saw it as a symbol of our developing friendship.

I wore the necklace at dinner that night. My whole family thought it was a strange gift from a carpenter to a homeowner. The girls' eyes were narrowed in suspicion. I defended Ed's motives in giving it to me. I defended my innocence in wearing it. That afternoon, after I put the necklace on, I made tea and Ed and I moved to my front porch. As he sipped his tea, his hands were shaking so violently I was afraid he would spill it.

We made polite chatter. Then Ed said, "I felt that I should tell you something." He cleared his throat, clearly uncomfortable. "I'm… I'm falling in love with you." Just like that.

There was no air or time between his words and my response: "I think I love you too, but *I'm* happily married." I had defined the boundaries. We chatted about what was on the CDs and about his next job, and then he left.

He continued to call me on my cell phone. We had agreed, without using the word "boundaries," that phone calls would be okay, but six or seven phone calls later, I told Ed they had to stop. I was finally aware of the depths of my own attraction, and what I really wanted was to talk for hours and hours. I wanted to hear Ed's stories. I wanted to tell him mine. I wanted contact. I longed.

"Bonni," I said one afternoon in September. "I'm worried."

I cried for days, then finally I took myself to a therapist. Less than a month after I told my friends I would never leave — and meant it — I made plans to move into an apartment across the street.

In my first session with Lorraine, I told her I had fallen in love with the carpenter. In the second session, she asked me to talk about my marriage. I said it was safe and comfortable, and I heard the emptiness in those bland adjectives. I was thinking about all the nights I spent lying in bed, awake at 3 a.m., crying over a deep unhappiness. I confessed that I had felt this way for most of my marriage. I believed that God used Ed to unlock my soul, to release me.

I told Lorraine about things I had told no one, like the day I'd watched Sally with her boyfriend and felt jealous of her excitement. I told her that movies with a romantic theme made me cry because I knew I would never experience that kind of passion again. I had known passion with a man I loved in college, but passion was not a factor in my marriage. I was in love with Bill when I married him. I knew that was important, but I was also seeking a stable provider, a family man, a good father. I was 22 when I made my choice. What did I know then about the intricacies of romance and emotional intimacy? What did I know about the need in a marriage for emotional and physical passion and connection?

In that 50 minutes in Lorraine's office, a sunny room where aloe plants and tissue boxes sat on every surface, I'd come to terms with the fact that I was not happily married. In fact, I was drowning. I needed to rescue myself. I needed to look at who I'd become and move toward who I wanted to be.

I wanted to be an adoring wife. I wanted to be adored. I wanted not to be me. I knew then that if I had been happily married I would not have fallen in love with the carpenter. I knew I needed to leave my husband, but not for Ed.

For me.

On the night that we told the girls that I was moving out, Sally cried, and Molly moaned and wailed, clinging to me as if I had just told her I was dying. That night, and every night until I moved, I slept on the sofa bed in my office. Angus, the dog, was the only creature who came through the door to say goodnight.

On the day I left, I was careful to fill the holes I was creating. I moved a couch from my studio in Florence, where I taught writing classes to children, to the living room to replace my parents' couch, which I was taking. Where I removed a picture, I hung another in its place, I was trying to create the illusion that nothing had changed when, in fact, everything had.

My husband's reaction to my decision changed from day to day. He was heartbroken. He agreed that our marriage had flaws. He was worried about the finances of divorce. He thought I was exhausted from the marathon training and that I should rest and think about what I was doing. One day, after I'd told him for the first time that I was in love with Ed, he was angry, and in the kitchen, he spat furious words at me. I was attracted to that raw emotion, but his feelings, and mine, passed.

In the still of my new apartment, after I had talked with my children on the telephone to say goodnight, and then talked to Ed for over an hour as well, God's was the only voice telling me that things would be alright. God, in fact, seemed to be the only steady presence in my life. I prayed for forgiveness for breaking my family apart. I prayed for healing for Bill and the girls, and I gave thanks for the gift of Ed.

Through the thin walls, I heard my neighbors climb the stairs. I heard their children arguing with one another. I heard Molly's little friend practice her violin. And I cried. I had broken my girls' hearts, and I missed them. Somehow, though, I still knew I was doing the right thing, Ed or not.

Chapter Three

I'm not sure who got back in touch with whom first. But I do remember that Ed was shocked when I told him I was moving out of my house. He was frightened I wasn't thinking things through. He was guilt-ridden.

"Are you sure you know what you're doing?" he asked me. He confessed to being in what he described as a dark, unhappy marriage, and he told me that he and his wife lived separately in the same home, but he was clear that he would not be moving out.

He went so far as to call Bonni. "Do you think it would help Janice if I disappeared from the picture?" he asked her.

"It's too late for that," she told him.

Even my husband said, "You can't put the toothpaste back in the tube."

The Episcopal Diocese of Western Massachusetts was among my clients at this time in my life. I wrote, edited and designed its magazine, the *Pastoral Staff*. I was expected to attend weekly meetings on Wednesdays, and over the course of the last few months, I had missed many. The woman I reported to, a priest, called me into her office one Wednesday and asked me what was going on. It all came out in a rush.

"I'm having trouble at home," I said. I started to cry. "I fell in love with the carpenter who renovated our kitchen. I'm moving out. He's married."

"Have you spoken to the bishop about this?"

"No," I said, the significance of the situation beginning to resonate. "Is this going to affect my job?"

"You need to talk to the bishop."

I made an appointment with him. On the day of our meeting, I spent the 25-minute car ride to his office planning what I would say — that I was captivated, that I'd gone to a therapist, that I was about to move out, that I was so happy for the first time in 16 years, that I planned to date this married man as soon as I had moved, that Ed's wife and my husband did not object, that Ed and I hadn't had an affair.

I spilled out my story in the bishop's office through tears of embarrassment and shame. The bishop was a kind and gentle man. He was in his late 50s, early 60s with thick white hair and a full white beard and mustache, like Santa's.

The bishop nodded as he listened. My goal was twofold: to keep my job, which I loved — who would not love telling stories of people in service to God? — and to receive permission to date Ed. I desperately wanted the bishop's blessing, so that I could follow my heart and feel that God really had had a hand in things.

When I told the bishop that I was leaving my husband and that I planned to start dating Ed soon afterwards, he asked me not to do so. He said marriage vows are in place until a couple is divorced. He was firm, but so was I.

"I can't wait," I told him.

I don't remember his final response, frankly. I only remember that even though he was emphatic in asking me to wait, he did not tell me I had to or give me an ultimatum.

He did say a prayer that went like this: "Dear Lord, watch over Janice, our sister in Christ, and guide her as she moves into a new chapter in her life. Allow her to feel the spirit of your guidance."

I already did.

After I moved, Ed and I talked on our cell phones almost constantly. We talked about our childhoods, high school, what we did that day. We talked about the bittersweet nature of our relationship, the sorrow in coming to the end of our marriages. He told me the plan for his own separation and asked me to be patient and respect that his process would take a lot longer than mine.

Ed and I did not talk about what our partners had done wrong in our marriages. We began to examine what *we* had done wrong and how we might do better next time. We talked about the fact that we hoped that "next time" would mean "us." We could not get enough of each other. My cell phone bill that first month of marital separation was $1,656. I borrowed money from my brother Allan to pay it and increased my minutes.

It was the end of October 2002 when I moved. I remember telling my mother I wouldn't invite Ed into my apartment behind my neighbor's house for a good long time. But by mid-November Ed was coming over for tea. Angus would become inconsolably excited, wagging his tail, wiggling all about, knocking things down because he had come to know Ed during the summer, and he knew that where there was Ed, there were treats. He'd gobble his treats down, and then, noticing that I had buried my head in Ed's neck, in his soft hair, Angus would bark. He would bark and bark and bark until we separated.

His reaction was not unlike the reactions of the people around us. No one was happy for us. Not our children, our families, our friends, our communities. We had become the kind of people who get whispered about on the sidewalk in front of Cooper's Corner.

I had been the unofficial social director in my neighborhood. I held parties for new neighbors. I had a party for the mailman when he retired. People came to me to borrow an egg or a box of pasta. They came for advice, a hug, hand-me-down children's clothing, but overnight, I imagined, I became simply "the woman who ran off with the carpenter."

Many people assumed we'd been carrying on all summer long in my Beacon Street house. I imagine they said, "No wonder that project took so long." But they were wrong.

Ed was accustomed to listening to his own strong and very stubborn heart, but it was the first time in my life that I gave up my need for social approval. My need for Ed was stronger.

Only four people were happy for us: Ed's mother, Peg; his father, also named Ed, who did not have long to live; my longtime and dear friend Judy, who had already seen me through many life changes; and Bonni.

"Dates" with Ed were tea dates, often at Cumberland Farms because it had decaf Lipton, Ed's favorite. He would go in while I waited in my car or his truck. We sipped our teas while driving on country roads, while watching Angus chase a tennis ball in the park, sitting on a blanket we'd spread on the grass. In those moments, we could forget that our children were in pain, that life was as much a struggle as it was a pleasure. We mused about our passions — his for music, mine for running and dance. We talked about who the disciplinarians were in our families, growing up — his father, my mother — and how we struggled to be firm with our own children, often allowing sentiment to get in the way of good sense. We talked about how long it might take to create a blended family. I saw this as something that was entirely possible, but Ed couldn't see how we were ever going to get there. His pessimism frustrated me and attracted me at the same time. I was learning that Ed saw most glasses as half empty, and I saw every glass as more than half full. We were Yin and Yang, we were learning, but that didn't matter. Ed was as adoring as my mother or father. He was as fun as my silliest girlfriends. And he listened with his whole heart, for the things that count.

In the fall of 2002, Ed was working on a job near downtown Northampton, and our tea "dates" moved to the King Street Cumberland Farms. One afternoon, I went there without him. At the hot drink station, I found the box of decaf Lipton and wrote, "I love you Ed," on its side in hopes he would spot it the next time he was in. I was 15 again.

Others saw this transformation in me, too. They saw it as regression.

I'd lost about 10 or 15 pounds over the summer. I'd been running at least 20 miles a week, training for the marathon in Maine, and I'd dropped to a size 2, the same size I had been in high school. At Molly's school bus stop, a neighbor told me, without kindness, that I looked like a "teenaged hippie." I was wearing bell-bottom jeans and black, platform shoes. I didn't feel like a hippie, but I did feel like a teenager again, and it felt good.

Six months later, only days after I'd put an offer on a house a mile away, this same neighbor asked me, "When are you moving?"

I thought he knew I'd made the offer, and I said, "I think in April. I just put the deposit down."

He said, "It's about time you moved out of the neighborhood. How do you think your husband feels watching your *boyfriend* drive by all the time?"

I was stung, but all I said was, "I think he's not quite as angry as you."

In March 2003, I attended the Diocesan Wardens and Vestry Gathering, a day-long workshop for leaders in the 67 churches of the Episcopal Diocese of Western Massachusetts. My job was to take notes, take pictures, and tell the stories of the day on the pages of the *Pastoral Staff* newsletter.

That day, the bishop talked about the need for congregations to consider modifying their operations to adapt to a changing world and a changing economy. He noted that changes to consider could be as substantial as parishes merging together to combine resources. He said sometimes Deep Change is necessary in the church. The alternative, he said, is Slow Death, and he encouraged congregations to choose the painful option of Deep Change rather than accepting Slow Death simply because that alternative is more comfortable.

Sometimes change is necessary, he said, and we all need to learn to adapt to it.

I took this as one more sign that God was on my side.

During this time, I prayed often, mostly while I was running. I'd recite the Lord's Prayer, and I prayed for people who I knew were sick. I prayed for comfort for my daughters, and I prayed for forgiveness — that I could forgive myself.

While I had no trouble praying, I found it difficult to go to church. I imagined everyone at St. John's knew I had left my husband for the carpenter.

Ed's wife moved out in July 2003. He threw out clothing and furniture, cleaned and redecorated, and then he invited me over for dinner. Still, another year passed before Ed and I began to spend nights together. It was not in my nature to be patient, but with Ed, I had to be. While I was ready to fully introduce Ed into my girls' lives, Ed wasn't ready to bring me into his sons' world. He insisted we continue to move slowly to give our children time to recover. This was something we argued over, but we argued as well as we did anything. It was safe to get angry, to voice concerns, to hotly disagree. This is how I learned that it was possible to have unconditional love for someone who was not my child. I loved Ed even though he would not do things my way. I learned to have respect for his way.

Eventually, I did finally begin to spend occasional weekends at Ed's house in Hatfield, Massachusetts, which he built when he was 25, using a book as a guide. It was camp-like, similar to my parents' house on Lake Winnisquam, and being there was private and freeing.

The property had once been Ed's grandfather's and was up the hill from the farmhouse he stayed in as a child when his father served in the Korean War. It was thickly wooded, overlooking gardens and fields, and from the living room window there was a beautiful view of Great Pond below.

Ed heated with wood, and his house smelled like wood smoke and the Nag Champ incense he liked to burn. The house was small, cozy and quaint, but his bed-room, which he'd added years after building the main house, was un-insulated and cold, sometimes only 40 degrees on a winter morning. It didn't matter to us because we spent those mornings in bed, under heavy blankets, warming each other. Ed and I could talk nonstop.

One morning, Ed recounted an already familiar story about his best friend, Bob, who had died of cancer.

"Bob used to give his wife Mind Gifts," Ed said. "He'd be somewhere, in a store, and he'd see something she would like, and he either didn't have the money for it or he thought it was only something she would like for a minute, or for a laugh. So, he'd go home and tell her, 'I have a Mind Gift for you.' And he'd tell her about what he saw."

I was caressing Ed's chest, feeling the hairs against the palm of my hand, feeling the vibration of his voice as he talked. While I had been listening to him, I was also daydreaming about a boyfriend I'd had in college who'd asked me, when I broke up with him, what it was I was looking for in a man.

I didn't have an answer then, but now, lying next to Ed, I knew I'd been looking for passion and mutual respect and connection.

I pecked Ed on the cheek.

"Here's a Mind Gift for you," I said. "You are what I've always wanted. I couldn't live without you."

Chapter Four

Not everything with Ed was like something out of a fairy tale. The relationship was something we worked hard at. It was real, full of the challenges that life and living in relationship present.

I learned that Ed battled an anxiety disorder that resulted in panic attacks and insomnia. I learned that this anxiety led Ed to drink Mr. Boston's blackberry brandy. After regularly spending nights with Ed, I also learned that Ed was not just taking the edge off with alcohol, the way I did. He was marinating in it, and this meant that I would have the opportunity to save his life.

Late in 2006, Ed was sick for months, his abdomen slowly expanding. He was nauseous and fatigued. He began to bleed from his nose and mouth, and then one day, I noticed the whites of his eyes turned yellow. He was in absolute and deep denial that his liver was failing, but I was able to convince him to let me take him to the emergency room at Cooley Dickinson Hospital in Northampton, Massachusetts.

"If you don't want to stay, you don't have to," I told him.

He was admitted, and he was told that if he drank again, he would be dead in six months. Ed had his last brandy on February 16, 2007. A heavy drinker myself at that point, I quit in solidarity.

The devastation that the withdrawal from alcohol brought on Ed was unexpected for both of us. He was fatigued, weakened and constantly sick to his stomach, and the lack of alcohol also profoundly affected his brain. We learned firsthand about a well-known syndrome called Post-Acute Withdrawal Syndrome, or PAWS.

Ed had trouble forming thoughts, making decisions, remembering anything. Literally unable to care for himself, Ed moved in with the girls and me, into the house I bought in 2003 on North Maple Street in Florence.

Ed was unable to work and, thus, forced to sell his Hatfield home. It was great to be living with him, but it was also our darkest hour. Ed was beaten, broken, and he was removed from his sons because there was no room for them to stay at my house, so he rarely saw them.

It took us months to find a new home, but it was worth the wait. It was in Easthampton, Massachusetts, and it was perfect. In addition to having a garage that could serve as a shop for Ed, it had a beautiful yard, complete with gazebo, and room for all the children to have their own space.

We moved in in August 2007. Finally, Ed and I had a house. The children were accepting. Ed was healthy. Finally, we were becoming a family.

On the day we got married, September 6, 2008, forecasters were predicting a hurricane, so we abandoned our plans for an outdoor ceremony on the gazebo and got married in a small building on our property that was once a store called the Hitching Post. Ed's youngest son Lee played the piano. My brother Allan, commissioned by the state of Massachusetts to be a justice of the peace for that day, led us through the vows. My brother Jeff made lasagna and shrimp cocktail and salads. My longtime friend, Judy, who had been the maid of honor the first time I was married and was there when both my children were born, was there, too, as was Bonni. Our entire family was there.

Sally was expecting a baby, and she was living with Tommy, the father. Ed's middle son, Riley and his girlfriend, Kisha, were expecting, too. Lee was in college. Jack, Ed's oldest son, had graduated from journalism school and was experimenting with careers. Molly was still in high school, wondering what her career might be. Ed and I loved watching our children grow up. We loved to watch them experimenting with how we all fit together. We couldn't wait to be grandparents and raise babies together because it was all going to be new, for all of us.

Everyone said it was good luck to get married in a hurricane. We believed them.

That first year in the house in Easthampton, Massachusetts, was our best year together. Ed was healthy. We loved to work together in the yard – me tending flower beds and mowing the lawn, Ed pruning trees and planting vegetables like cucumbers and tomatoes. After a hard day's work, we'd walk around the yard with a cup of tea and show each other the work we'd done. We were so supportive and proud of each other.

One chilly night in early spring, a cold, heavy rain was beating down on the house and the deck. I was in my usual evening position on the couch; Ed in his — his yellow chair. We were watching an episode of "CSI," and Grissom was studying the bugs on a decomposing body to estimate time of death.

Then there was a pounding on the back door, and we startled.

"Honey. You get it, okay?" I said. I was actually frightened, even in our safe neighborhood, tucked in our safe home.

Ed rose and flipped the outside light on and opened the door. The rubber weather stripping on the bottom scraped across the tile.

"Is Neil here?" I heard a male voice ask. I was crouched on the couch, listening.

"I'm sorry. I think you have the wrong house," Ed said.

"Neil used to live here. I grew up across the street," the voice said. "He lived here then."

"Okay," Ed said. "I'm afraid he doesn't live here anymore."

"Well, I need some help," the man voice said. "It's pouring, and I live in my car, and we're out of gas, and my buddy and I are freezing. Could you lend us a few dollars for gas, so the heater will run?"

"Come on in," Ed said. I didn't move.

As it turns out, the man was really not much more than a boy. He told us his parents had kicked him out of the house and that he'd been living in the town shelter in Easthampton, but recently got tossed out of there as well.

I was alarmed, but Ed took pity on this lost soul, dripping water onto the tile and shivering. He asked the boy for his wet sweatshirt, and he put it in the dryer. Then Ed padded upstairs and changed into jeans while the boy waited. He brought down his favorite sweatshirt.

"Here. You can have this," he said.

Ed went with the boy to the Pride station down the street and filled his gas tank and bought him a hot coffee and a sandwich, plus one for his equally lost friend. When they had gone, Ed settled back in his chair and pulled the scratchy grey wool blanket over him.

"That was really nice, honey," I said.

He looked at me in earnest. "That's what I'd want someone to do for my boys if they were in trouble, even if they brought it on themselves."

Ed had been struggling more than usual with the memory and cognitive problems that still occasionally plagued him as a result of the alcoholism. This is how I was given the chance to save his life a second time.

I'd come home from my job in the marketing department at Cooley Dickinson Hospital, a full-time job I had while still operating Beetle Press part time, and Ed would be searching for his cell phone or his date book or his car keys. I noticed that even simple, routine tasks were beyond him, and I suggested he go see his doctor, but stubborn as usual, he did not.

Then one day, Ed went out for a cup of tea and ran out of gas and didn't know how to get home. He called me, confused and shaken, from his cell phone, and I called his neurologist to give him details on what was happening.

"Get him to the emergency room. It's his liver," the doctor said, and I thought he was crazy.

"No," I said. "It's his brain."

"Yes, his brain is toxic. It's from the cirrhosis," he told me. "It can be fatal. It's an emergency. Go now."

I had to argue with Ed to get him to go to Cooley Dickinson. He was so confused and disoriented he didn't believe there was even a problem, let alone a serious one. He was admitted for a week-long stay. He was given a prescription drug that removed or neutralized the ammonia that had built up in his brain. He was able to keep track of everyday things once again, but it became clear, at least to me, that he would never be able to work again.

While Ed didn't work outside the house, he worked tirelessly around it, and he took on such tasks as the laundry and shopping. We had a routine that did not waver from day to day.

Every weekday began at 6:08 a.m., when my alarm would go off. Every eight minutes, the snooze button would jolt me again, and after I was awake, I'd roll over into Ed's arms, and we'd hold one another and share our dreams from the night before. At 6:45 a.m., when Molly got up for school, I got up for work. Ed got up with us. He made breakfast and packed a lunch for Molly.

While I got dressed, Ed made us tea. In winter, he'd start my car and Molly's to let them warm up, and he'd scrape our windshields. Molly left first, in a blur of food and backpack, and when I put my coat on, Ed would walk me out and carry my tea. If it was raining, he held an umbrella over me.

"I love you, honey," I would tell him before I drove away.

"More every day," he would say.

While I was designing brochures and fliers and writing testimonials for the hospital's website, Ed was at home, fixing things and restoring antiques. When I got home, Ed was always still working. Often, he was covered in grease or paint or oil. He would stop what he was doing, boil water and make us tea.

At the dinner table, sometimes just Ed and Molly and I, sometimes with Sally and her newborn son, Eli, too, we'd talk about the day, who we saw, what we did, what annoyed us, what made us happy. Later, Ed and I would settle in for a crime show.

As it had begun, the day would end with the two of us in each other's arms.

Ed would tell me, "I really do love you more every day. More. Every day." I could hear the wonder of it in his voice.

That's how it was before Ed was dying.

Chapter Five

One of Ed's hobbies had always been writing and recording his original songs, and he had recently renewed his focus on this area of his life, completing a new song called "On the County Line," about a laid-off factory worker who set out on the road to find a new life, beyond the county line. It was a beautiful song, but full of sadness, as were all of Ed's lyrics. They told stories about love sacrificed for the pull of the road and the promise of stardom.

"Why don't you write a song about me, honey?" I would ask every so often. "You can write a love song with a happy ending."

"I'm just not sure I could," he would tell me. "But I'll try."

In February or March 2010, Ed decided to record "On the County Line." He interviewed several female vocalists and settled on a woman named Dale. He sent her his music and set a date to record.

I loved watching the energy Ed put into his music and the thrill it gave him to be creative and follow this passion. On the day he and Dale went to the recording studio, I couldn't wait for him to come home to tell me how the session had gone. I was in the bathtub when I heard his footfalls downstairs, and I called him up.

The look on his face when he walked in the steamy bathroom told me things had not gone as planned.

"What happened?" I asked him. "How did it go?"

"Terrible," he said.

He sat down on the floor, pulled his knees up to his chest and told me that when Dale started to sing, there was no sound.

"She kept asking me to give her another minute, and she'd take a drink of water and try again, and when she was able to sing, it sounded awful. Not at all like she sounded on her own cuts," he said.

"I don't get it," I said. "Why?"

There was silence, and I could see that Ed was having difficulty telling this story. Since I am not good at waiting, I pestered.

"Well, what happened, honey? I'm confused."

"She asked if we could step into the sound room, alone. She was embarrassed that the studio guy was listening," Ed said. "When we got in the room, she told me she had multiple sclerosis, and that it was affecting her voice. She said some days she just can't sing, and she can't predict when it will happen."

"Oh God," I said.

"Yeah," he said. "It was awful."

"So what did you do?"

"We packed up, and she asked me if she could try again with me. She said she loves my tunes, but I had to pay $100 for the time today, and we didn't get any tracks down. I can't do that again. Is that cruel?" he asked me. "It's not her fault."

"No, honey. It's not cruel, and it's not her fault, but it's not yours either. I think it's okay to find somebody else."

"Yeah, I just don't have the money for that kind of delay."

And, as it turned out, Ed also did not have the time.

In the fall of 2009, Sally and Eli were living with us, along with Molly. Our house was busy and full.

Ed battled pneumonia that summer and was hospitalized for several days. I stayed with him as much as I could. Alone in his room at Cooley Dickinson, in the new patient wing with fancy televisions and a fold-out futon for guests, we snuggled in his bed and marveled at the quiet without the girls and Eli under foot.

"I feel like we're on vacation," I told him.

When Ed's treatment was complete, and he was back home, it seemed he was tired all the time.

My parents were selling the camp on Lake Winnisquam, and one weekend, we went to visit and help them pack. Ed carried musty boxes from the cellar and helped my parents decide what to discard.

"Ed shouldn't be doing this," my mother whispered to me, knowing he'd only been out of the hospital a few weeks.

"He's fine, Mom," I said.

And I did think he was fine. But, a few months later, I noticed the trash building up in our shed. I noticed, too, that Ed was not as quick to ask Molly at night what she wanted for breakfast. He even slept in one morning, and I kissed him, warm under the covers, and said I would see him at the end of the day, but when I got home, he was napping on the couch.

Several more months passed. Ed talked about his thighs hurting constantly. I thought it was overwork, maybe pulled muscles, or even rheumatoid arthritis. No big worry, in other words, but time to see a physician.

Dr. Katz took X-rays of Ed's lungs, which surprised us. He said he was following up on the pneumonia. We didn't get the connection. We were focused on Ed's leg pain. It's what bothered him the most, wore him out. But Dr. Katz said he saw something on that X-ray that hadn't been there before and ordered a biopsy.

Less than 24 hours later, I was driving on the interstate to Molly's lacrosse game when my cell phone rang.

It was Dr. Katz. My heart started to race.

"Janice, the results of some of our tests are in," he told me. There was a pause that frightened me because it meant he was not ready to speak the words, and I wasn't ready to hear them.

"Ed has lung cancer."

I struggled to keep my car on the road.

"Lung cancer?" I was crying. "His pain is in his *thighs*."

"The cancer has spread to his lymph nodes in his chest and, we suspect, to areas of bone," Dr. Katz told me. There was compassion in his voice, but he was unapologetic, straightforward. "The pain he is feeling in his legs — that is likely from tumors. We'll have to do a PET-CT to know more."

"No," I said. "No, no, no." Over and over "no." I sounded like Eli, 9 months old now.

Dr. Katz said consoling things, but I escalated. "So, what do we *do*?" I was wailing, and I was thankful the bus carrying Molly and the rest of the team was still in front of me, that it was so large and yellow. It served as both a buffer between my daughter and me and a beacon that I followed.

"The disease is treatable but not curable," he told me.

"What does that mean?" Even little pieces were impossible to process.

"Surgery is not possible, but chemotherapy might do some good. I think we're looking at a lifespan of a few months to a year." His voice was neutral.

"A few months?" I tried to listen as he described the next steps, and we hung up.

Then, in my car, I began to bellow. "No. No. No. God no. This can't be happening. This is *not* happening."

We had worked so hard to get to a place where life together was good, and it was so good. We had all worked hard, sacrificed, suffered. How could this be how it would end? How could this be?

I moaned and keened and rocked. I could barely see, but I kept following that bus as if my own life depended on it.

I pulled into the playing fields and parked far from the bus, afraid for Molly to see me, afraid of what I had to tell her. I headed to the school's side door. I needed to go to the bathroom. I needed to blow my nose. I needed to call my husband, who still did not know.

The door was locked, so I knocked. Then I pounded. I rested one wet cheek on the pane of glass. My chest was heaving as if I had just run a 5K, and my hair was wet. I turned away, trying to figure out what I would do next, when the door was opened by what looked to be a young teacher. Several children were staring at me. They looked concerned.

"You look like you need help," the teacher said. "Do you want to come in?"

"I'd love to use the bathroom," I said.

"Do you want to come into my classroom and sit for a moment?"

I shook my head "no." I could not be trusted around children. I would scare them. I was so scared myself. I wanted to tell her what was happening, but I didn't want to speak the words. I didn't want to hear them or make them real.

In the bathroom, I blew my nose. Wiped my eyes. Took deep breaths. Regained some of my composure. Then my cell phone rang. It was Ed. I hurried back outside.

"My doctor called," he said. There was a long pause. "He said I have lung cancer."

"'I know," I wailed. "I know, honey." Ed was silent, so I filled in all the blanks in the conversation. "I'm so sorry, honey. I love you. I'm sorry I'm not with you. I wanted to tell you. I'm sorry I'm not with you." I repeated it over and over.

"What do we do?" he said. He sounded so frightened, so lost.

"Call an oncologist. And hope."

I could have gone home to him right then, but I wanted to stay. I wanted to set up my sports chair on the sideline and pretend to have one hour of normal life before it all fell apart. I told Ed I'd be home in a few hours, and he was okay with that. He had a lot of thinking to do, he said. I cried as we hung up.

I set my chair up on the field, away from all the other parents, and I continued to cry, but I focused on my daughter, her fierce face, her athletic body. Her perfectness. I had a thought, watching her, a thought that at that time I would tell no one: *I'm so glad it's not you. Not Sally. Not Eli.*

God was nowhere that day. There was only the yellow school bus, my daughter, and my Ed, my soul mate, waiting for me at home.

Chapter Six

Ed's illness brought my belief in God, in heaven, into sharp focus. Worrying about life without him reminded me that I had heard messages. It gave me an odd kind of hope.

I dwelled on the time back in high school that I had actually died, for a moment, and was pulled toward heaven. I had driven to a dance at a place called Blackburn Hall with my friends Lisa and Laurie and Laurie's boyfriend. He was 18 and stopped to get booze. I drank a half pint of rum, straight from the bottle.

When we pulled in the parking lot of the hall, Lisa opened the door to the truck, and I fell out onto the pavement.

"Beetle, what are you doing?" she said with a laugh. Then, when I didn't move, "Are you okay?"

Lisa walked me around the town common, and when my pulse slowed, she ran back to Blackburn Hall and found a senior who not only knew how to drive but also knew CPR. They picked me up, got me in the back seat of the car and drove me to the hospital. I would learn the next day that I wet my pants and also threw up in the car. I would also learn, from my parents, that the doctors lost my pulse and my heartbeat while they were pumping out my stomach. They said it was a miracle that I survived.

What I never told anyone back then, because it seemed like a dream as opposed to an actual experience, was that I saw myself dead. I was on the hospital table with a tube down my throat. Doctors were working over me, and then I sat up. I looked to my left, at a large mirror that covered the wall, and I could see myself. I was sitting up, looking in the mirror, but I was also lying on the table with a tube in my throat and my eyes closed. There was intense light coming from the mirror. It seemed to be beckoning. Come. Come. I leaned toward it, pulling with my arms, toward that beautiful light. It seemed to hold the promise of great joy. Then I lay back down.

I thought about that light now. I thought about Ed dying and moving into that safe, beautiful place. And I thought about the times when I'd channeled people who had died.

It started with my Great Aunt Barbara, who died in her 90s when I was in college. I'd come home one afternoon, and my mother motioned to a cardboard box on the kitchen table. She asked me to guess what was inside. I ran my hands through what felt like tiny bits of shell or coral and said I didn't know.

"It's your Aunt Barbara," she said.

"Gross," I said, and we laughed.

Ten years later, though, when Aunt Barbara was still sitting on a metal shelf in the garage of the camp in that plain white box, I didn't think it was funny anymore. Aunt Barbara didn't either. In a dream, she came to me and repeated, over and over, "Take me home. Take me home. Take me home." I didn't see her face, and the voice I heard wasn't hers, but when I woke up, I knew what needed to be done.

I had memories of Aunt Barbara reading the Bible in the bed next to mine on Christmas Eve and the day before Easter, and I knew she was a devout Christian Scientist. I told my parents about the dream and told them that Aunt Barbara wanted to be buried so she could rest in heaven. They listened to me, and they spread her ashes where her parents were buried, near my brother Johnny.

Ed knew this story, and he knew that I had had conversations with other people who were dead, like my good friend Robyn, who died of brain cancer. Robyn came to me on the lacrosse field, when her daughter Samantha was playing on a team with Molly and asked me to watch Samantha. She said she could see her through my eyes. I loved that notion, and I began to watch both girls on the field each time they played. Ed also knew that a day after my friend Judy's brother-in-law died, while I was running, he came to me and asked me to tell his wife that he was okay.

Then there was the time I was cooking dinner and reached for a spoon in the ceramic canister next to the stove. What my fingers landed on in the tangle of spatulas and tongs was a gold-plated spoon that had once belonged to my late cousin David and his late partner, Emmanuel.

"That is so weird," I called out to Ed. He was sitting in his yellow chair in the living room. He looked up at me.

"I just talked to David when I was running. I hadn't even thought of him in a very long time, and while I was running and praying, well, there he was in my head, and now, I'm standing here holding his spoon."

Ed didn't exactly believe these encounters I had, but he didn't ridicule or discount them either. He was keeping his judgment in check, just in case. And that was good because when we found out Ed was dying, he needed my faith as much as I did. We were both counting on my prayers to keep him alive.

I prayed, and I prayed.

I prayed when we woke up in the morning and I rolled over to wrap my arms around him. "Please, God, do not take this man away from me. Let him live a long, wonderful life." I prayed at my desk at Cooley Dickinson Hospital. "Please, please, please." I prayed over my lunch of ham and cottage cheese, and when I ran, I recited the Lord's Prayer, singing it as I had when I was a kid. I prayed as we watched television and he fell asleep in his chair. "Please God, I can't live without this man. Please heal him. Please don't take him away." I prayed when, in bed for the night, we held each other before we started to nod off. "I will never sleep again without him. Please, God. Please don't take him."

I prayed silently, and I prayed out loud. I was counting on God, but there came a point when I knew God could not answer my prayers any more than he could answer prayers to win the lottery or stop the war. So I started praying for comfort for Ed. I prayed that he would one day see that beautiful light and know that God was bringing him home.

I didn't tell Ed this. We couldn't bring ourselves to talk about what was happening. It was far too painful.

I did ask Ed, though, over and over, to find me from the other side.

"I will hear you. Please, honey, find me."

Ed said he would, but I could see in his eyes that he was afraid he wouldn't know how.

In June 2010, Ed and I bought a notebook and made a list of the things he wanted to do before he died. As he grew weaker, as he weathered chemotherapy, radiation, hospital stays for transfusions; we tried our best to have fun. We took long drives around the Valley. We'd stop for a tea and sit alongside Nashawannuck Pond or watch the horses in the field near our house.

We spent several days with Sally, Molly and Eli at my brother Jeff's house on Lake Winnipesaukee. We visited Lee and went to his first gig in New York City with a band called The Druthers. We visited Ry, Kisha and their baby son Emmett, only a few months younger than Eli. We went to see the movie "Inception," and we both fell asleep. We took his mother to the carousel at a local park. We went to a firing range, and Ed taught me how to shoot his handgun. We each fired off 20 rounds, and he hit his target only once. When I took Ed to the Bridge of Flowers in Shelburne Falls in late August, and he needed me to pick him up in the car after we walked the quarter mile across the bridge to the other side, I knew Ed was really going to die.

I had already faced the fact that we had made love for the last time. Now, I realized that we'd spent our last Christmas together. That we had gone on our last walk, shared our last Valentines. That we would not teach our grandchildren to press cider or take them trick-or-treating. That we would never play board games in a summer camp on the water in our retirement.

At times, Ed seemed to know this too, but we only talked about it in snippets, when our grief overtook the part of us that protected the other. Like the time Ed was lying on the couch, silent.

"Are you okay, honey?" I asked him.

"I think we need a video camera," he said. His face was drawn, and he was crying. I moved over to hold him in my arms.

"How else will Emmett remember me?"

And there were times I would cry and tell him, "You can't leave me, honey. I can't live without you," but he would say, "I'm not going anywhere."

Ed was diagnosed about eight months after Sally moved out of our house with Eli, at our request. We wanted her to be independent. We felt she might not learn how to care for Eli on her own if she wasn't on *her* own.

The therapist we'd been seeing while they lived with us, Melissa, had walked with us through the excruciating decision-making and Sal's actual move. When Ed was diagnosed with cancer, Melissa became the person who walked us through grief. She helped us with the most difficult decisions — when to begin my family medical leave, what items to put on Ed's bucket list, how to talk to each other about what was happening to us.

"Ed asked me to promise I would never be with another man."

I say this in a rush to Melissa in the middle of a session. I had told Ed I was going to bring it up because he had asked for this promise several times, and I could not answer. I did not know the right answer.

Melissa asked me, "And how do you feel about that?"

I couldn't look at Ed. "I can't make that promise because I don't know if I can keep it."

Then, I looked at Ed, who was crying, and I told him this: "I love you more than I have ever loved any man. You are my soul mate. I can't imagine that I could ever find a man I would love as much as I love you. But I can't promise you that I won't."

Melissa asked Ed why the promise from me was so important to him.

"I don't want anyone to be with Janice when I can't."

When Ed and I married, I did not take his name. After the divorce, it had been difficult for me to transition from my married name back to my maiden name, Janice Beetle, and I didn't want to transition again. Ed never tried to talk me into being a Godleski, but I knew he would have liked it.

There wasn't much I could do for him now. I could keep him comfortable with morphine. I could place cool cloths on his forehead. I could lie with him. But I could

41

not take away his pain. He was losing sight of himself. In desperation, he would ask, "Do you still love me?"

I didn't know how to show him just how very much.

But then I had an idea. I went to the registry and got a new driver's license that read Janice Beetle Godleski. I took that license to the bank, and I got new checks that read Janice Beetle Godleski.

At home, Ed was on the couch. "What've you been doing, Janice?" he asked me.

I sat on the piano stool inches away from his face.

"This," I said, handing him my new license and checks.

He started to cry.

I began a family medical leave from my job when Ed was hospitalized on the Fourth of July. We had hoped that he might live another year, maybe more, until the day Dr. Smith told us that the chemotherapy had not worked. After three treatments, some tumors had shrunk, but there were new tumors, a lot of them. Ed was dying. He asked, "How long?"

The answer was months, weeks. But really, Dr. Smith did not know. Tears were slipping down Ed's cheeks, but he wouldn't look at me.

My friends knew that, without my hospital income, making mortgage payments was going to be difficult. Two of them hosted a fundraiser at their home in Hatfield, and musicians that Ed had played with performed songs he had written over the years. His three sons came and played together — Ry on the drums, Jack on bass and Lee on guitar — all three singing to their father, singing his songs.

Ed pushed Emmett around the party in his stroller, leaning on it for support. He greeted old friends, his first wife, her brother. He was the life of the party.

That was August 28, 2010.

Ed had lost so much weight that I could count his ribs. The freckle that was tucked inside the swell of his buttocks was visible because there was no swell any longer. Ed lost so much weight his wedding ring fell off, and we had to put it in a box on his dresser. He kept talking about "when I get stronger," yet he wouldn't eat.

I made his favorite soups. I made fruit smoothies. I made him root beer floats. For days, he ate nothing. He continued to lose weight. He got weaker, frailer. He looked 90 years old.

In the doctor's office, I asked for tips on getting Ed to eat.

"Don't make him eat if he doesn't want to," she told me.

I think that's when my mind went dark.

I started taking Ed's Ativan, prescribed for anxiety.

Daily activities shrank to the confines of our house. My view of the world became fuzzy and dream-like. I lacked peripheral vision and could see only what was in front of me.

My mind processed information on a triage basis:

Measure morphine.

Put a cold cloth on Ed's head.

Are his feet covered?

We celebrated our second wedding anniversary on September 6, 2010, by taking a nap on the couch.

The next day, Ed could no longer climb the stairs to get to our bedroom. We called Hospice, and they brought a hospital bed and an oxygen tank into our living room.

Then the house filled with family. Jack and his girlfriend, Louise, came from their apartment in Northampton. Lee and his girlfriend, Ana, came from Brooklyn. Sally and Eli stayed with us, too.

On Thursday, my boss called to tell me my job at the hospital was eliminated. I was being laid off. I know I responded, made conversation on the phone, but I was lost, disappearing.

That night, Ed fell down in the middle of the night, trying to get to the bathroom. Lee and Jack raced up from the basement and, together, they were able to help Ed get back into bed.

Measure morphine. Put a cold cloth on Ed's head. Make dinner for seven.

Take Ativan. Sleep.

On Friday, Ry came with Kisha and Emmett. Ed patted Emmett's head. He loved to feel Emmett's tight ringlet curls. That night, I lay in his bed and read notes that Sally and Molly wrote for him. They told him they loved him. Molly thanked him for being like a father to her. I whispered to Ed, "Don't forget to find me, honey. Come find me." He couldn't respond. He was not sleeping; he was unconscious.

I retreated further inside my head.

There were many visitors. Judy, Ed's best friend, Kelly, his wife, Kate. My friend Bonni with her daughter Ali. They were saying goodbye. It all seemed normal, if you didn't focus on the reality.

Boil water for tea. Measure morphine.

We took Ed out on the deck in a wheelchair to sit in the sun. He couldn't hold his head up. I held it between my hands at the base of his neck. I thought, "He is dying he's dying he's going. When? How much longer?"

Lie in Ed's bed. Do not touch him. It hurts.

On Monday, September 13, 2010, Ed lay unconscious in the living room. The children were gathered around. Everyone was quiet. Waiting.

Ed's breathing became thick, labored, horrifying. Our Hospice nurse, Eileen, told us that this was the end. Ed's lungs were filling with fluid. He was drowning. Eileen asked if a Hospice volunteer could come to give Ed a Reiki treatment.

"Yes, please," I told her.

Find a phone book. Choose a funeral home. Let the Hospice volunteer in.

Lee played the piano. I climbed in Ed's bed, aware of the efforts of the Hospice volunteer, whose head was inches from ours. Ry sat on the couch and held Ed's hand.

Peaceful. Love. Music. My family. Ed.

Then the volunteer left.

Say goodbye. Hug her.

She leaned in to my ear, "He loves you very much. I could feel it in his chakra."

Cry. Take more Ativan. Wonder if this really is happening.

Ask Ana and Louise to make dinner.

The house quieted at 10 p.m. Judy and I stayed with Ed in the living room, his breathing the only sound that could be heard. Judy agreed to take a shift caring for Ed until 2 a.m.

Take Ativan. Sleep. Block it all out.

Judy woke me at 2 a.m. and fell asleep on the futon on the living room floor.

Ed lifted his head at 2:40 a.m. He looked right into my eyes. He knew it was me.

I went to him, took his hand, and words came out, quiet but clear, in his ear: "It's okay, honey. You can let go now. We love you. We will always love you. And we will be okay. I promise. You can let go. But… find me."

Ed took several more breaths. Ed died. It was not real.

Wake Judy. Ask her if Ed really died. Is Ed dead?

I'm really not sure.

Judy is. She says he is gone.

How did this happen?

What do we do now?

Wake the children.

I crawled into bed with Ed to hold him one last time. His body was so frail, but I knew I could no longer hurt him.

Screech. Wail. Hold Ed as tight as I can.

Call Hospice. Call the funeral home. Take Ativan.

"In came the cold wind, the chill of reality. The one that I loved most of all wasn't meant to be."

– Edward M. Godleski,
from his song "Cold Wind"

Chapter Seven

Because we had talked about death long before Ed was sick, I knew he wanted to be cremated. He wanted half his ashes to be spread in the river, as his father's had, and he wanted the other half saved in an urn so that someday, half of my ashes could be placed with his.

Four days after he died, I follow through on his wishes. I weep as I place half his ashes in the ornamental urn that Judy, Molly and I found at a local antique store. The remaining ashes stay in the cardboard box the funeral director brought over. It looks just like the box my Aunt Barbara spent 10 years in.

On the weekend, we have a family memorial for Ed. I rent a party barge. My father drives my boat, and out on the river we go — my parents, Ed's mother, all five of our children and their partners, our two grandchildren, Ed's best friend and his wife and Judy. We idle up into Hatfield, where Ed had raised his family.

When we reach our destination, just north of the dike in Hadley, we tether the boats together, and everyone comes aboard the party barge. We are quiet, anxious, grieving.

The day is sunny and bright. I read the 23rd Psalm, noting that Ed wasn't a big believer in God but that he did honor green pastures, and then we take turns sharing a memory or telling a story and scooping a cupful of his ashes into the river as we do so. The ashes sound like sand hitting the water, and they drift quickly away.

Ed's sons talk about a father who was nurturing, attentive and competent. My father weeps recalling how Ed had called him to ask permission to marry me. I talk about a man who was patient and kind and who taught me how to love and be loved. The grandchildren, guided by their mothers, also take turns releasing Ed's ashes.

It was quiet when all of Ed was gone. We head back to the marina. When I return the party barge, I notice tiny bits of Ed's ashes on the rear platform. I want to wash them off myself, gently, but I can't bear to, so I walk away. I don't really understand yet that Ed is gone. It seems like we've had a family outing that he somehow missed.

That night, the children and I light a fire in the pit in our yard. Judy is with us. We sit close around the fire. I know that the next day we will break apart. I'm not ready.

Ana passes around rice paper and pens, and asks us to write down our wishes for Ed and then place the paper in the fire; she says because the paper is special, the ashes will make their way toward the heavens.

I fill my paper on both sides, asking Ed to please come back, to find me. Later, I realize that what I have written is all about what I need, so I take a second piece of paper and tell Ed I hope he is free of pain. I hope he is somewhere beautiful. I add that to the fire as well.

Then, as the rest of the group lifts in spirit, laughing, carousing, I slowly sink into sadness. They are all drinking; I am not. I have decided to wait six months before attempting to drink alcohol again.

I start to miss Ed in a crushing way. A piece of our family — a piece of me — is missing. I think, "If Ed were here, the boys would be out here enjoying themselves, and Ed and I would be inside, watching TV, loving each other and eating snacks before heading to bed." It is the first time I allow the fact that Ed is gone, that he will never be in his chair again, to slip into my mind. As soon as the thought comes, I shut it off. It is dangerous.

I am numb and need to be more numb. I smoke pot with the kids, but it only heightens my anxieties.

In the bathroom, as I look at my stoned, tear-stained face in the mirror, I hear Ed.

"You are a mess, Janice," he says. He is laughing.

"You found me, honey. You did it," I gasp. Then, "Where are you?"

But he is gone. Any good buzz I had evaporated. I say my goodnights and head to bed.

I sob, drool, blow my nose, and repeat over and over, "Ed is dead." Sometimes it is a question, sometimes a statement. I stare at a picture of him next to my dresser. In it, he is walking on the beach in Beverly, where Ry and Kisha live. He has Emmett on his back in a backpack. He looks sexy, handsome.

I talk at him in a long monologue that goes something like this: "Ed, you can't be gone. I need you. I need you. You are not dead. Come back. Please come back. Oh God. I can't do this. I can't. Ed, you are dead? How could that be? No, no, no. You have to come back. I can't do this without you."

Ed loved to take care of me. I feel him for a brief moment in my stupor. He tells me, "Janice, take an Ativan."

"Good idea, honey," I say. I take two. I cry until I fall asleep.

Chapter Eight

Ed's boys are gone and they have taken Kisha, Emmett, Louise and Ana with them. Judy is home in Somerville. Sally is at work, as is everyone I know who still has a job. Eli is at daycare. Molly is at school. I am in bed. I have no job, nowhere to go.

I spend much of my time planning how I could die because I am sure that if I die, I can be with Ed.

I sleep all day, and when I wake up, I take Ativan by the handful because I don't want to think. I don't want to be. There is nothing left. I am dying, and I am glad. When I have to get up, when Molly comes home from school, I realize I can move. I can speak. But I can't make dinner, and I can't eat. I am good at ordering takeout, and that's how we survive.

When Ed and I moved into our house, we placed a tiny porcelain figurine, a trinket that had been his grandmother's, on the window ledge in our bedroom. She became someone we talked about at night. We joked that she was working up the courage to jump, and we wondered if she intended to make it all the way to the bed or if her plan was simply to plunge to the wooden floor. I am that insignificant piece of folk art now. I am on the edge. I want to jump. I wonder who is watching to see if I'll really do it.

I think about what I could jump from. The Coolidge Bridge over the Connecticut River, but I don't think it's high enough to prove fatal. The library tower at the University of Massachusetts, but how would I get up there? I had a colleague at the Springfield newspaper who also worked in the library and had access to the roof. One day, she put on a black dress and a black veil and jumped off the building. Her husband, the police reporter, was one of the first people to find her.

I think I could jump off my own roof if I had the energy to drag the ladder out from under the deck and climb it, but that is just too much work. I think about swallowing all the medications that are left in the house. I have Ativan. There is Ambien, Oxycodone, Nyquil, anti-diarrheal, birth control, antacids. There is enough to mix together and poison myself, I am sure. But I don't do it. I sleep. I think about slitting my wrists in the bathtub, but that is too messy. I think about buying rum and stopping my heart like I did when I was 15.

I survive the first week without my husband by planning my death. My friends call every day to check on me. When I'm able to answer the phone, I don't tell them what consumes my thoughts.

All summer, Ed had worried that our studio building needed painting. Now I see that the garage needs painting too. The back seat in the boat has crumbled. The dishwasher will not close. The ceiling light in Molly's room is dim. Her radiator doesn't work. The leaves are starting to fall in our enormous yard. I am dying. I cannot manage this. I need Ed. Ed took care of everything.

I make a to-do list. It makes me feel I have some control over things, and I put the dishwasher at the top. I call Sears, and they send me Clif, with one "f." He comes at the end of the day. It's been a week since Ed died, but it feels like it's been much longer. I feel old.

When I called in the problem, I was clear with the dispatcher that the dishwasher won't close because it was installed improperly, so it moves around underneath the countertop. Yet when I show the problem to Clif, he tells me, "Oh, I don't have the tools to make this kind of repair. That's an installation problem."

I try my best to be calm. I think to myself, "Yes, that's why I called. Why didn't they tell you to bring the right fucking tools??"

Then Clif asks me, "Do you know anyone who is handy? Someone who can work with wood? They could fix this easily."

He knows not what he has done.

In a flash, I am wailing. "My husband was a carpenter. He could have fixed this. He had the tools. But he died. He just died. He is dead. That's why I needed to call you."

I am messy, unhinged, so I apologize and go to my office and check email. I hear Clif doing things, and he calls to me and repeats that he really can't fix it. When he is done with doing nothing, I have to pay him $110 for simply showing up. When I hand him the check, which reads "Janice Beetle Godleski, dba Beetle Press," Clif looks at it and asks, "How is it that so many people can work from home?" He thinks he is complimenting me, making me feel good. "I'd love to work from home."

He does not understand I have no job, no husband. I live in my bed. I have nothing.

I know it is time to clean out my office at Cooley Dickinson Hospital, so one afternoon I head over there. I defiantly wear jeans – against the rules for employees, but I am no longer an employee. I am one of several hundred laid off over the past 18 months.

I take the four flights of stairs from the basement entry, hoping no one sees me. I don't want anyone to talk to me about Ed, or, God forbid, ask how he is.

I turn the light on in my office and close the door. I lean against it. If I leave the door closed, I can imagine that I have a few brochures to crank out and that Ed is out grocery shopping and by the time I leave, he'll be home making dinner.

I start by taking my pictures off the walls, like the one of me talking to Bill Cosby after a press conference at UMass. I take down the framed cartoon from an artist I wrote about. Then I tackle the hard stuff — the family photos on my bulletin board. There is a picture of an 8-year-old Ed with short hair and his then-pointy ears. On the photo, he had written a note: "Will you be my Valentine?"

It is terrible work I am doing, erasing both of us from this room. Then, there's a knock on the door. My boss.

"Hi," she says, and I can tell she's wary. Will I yell at her? Cry? Storm out of the room? "How are you?"

"I'm OK. Just packing up," I say, stating the obvious.

"I'm so sorry," she says. "About everything."

"Yeah. Me, too."

She hands me something and says, "I found this. I knew you'd want it."

It's a small card, the kind you get with a bouquet from the florist. I see Ed's handwriting under the printed word "because": "you had a bad day, and I love you." I remember the day he came in here with a dozen red roses and left them on my desk because I was fighting with Sally.

I continue packing, and when I leave, I'm at a complete loss. I have nowhere else to go.

On Sunday, I invite Mary out on the boat. She has been my friend for roughly 20 years. Sally and her daughter Jo Jo were best friends as toddlers.

Mary and I head north to the Hadley dike. It is unseasonably warm for late September, and we sunbathe and go swimming. Early afternoon turns to twilight. We talk about Ed. We talk about nothing. We talk about war.

"Remember my student who went to Iraq and then shot herself?" Mary asks me.

I do remember. Mary had been quoted in a newspaper story about the death. "I didn't remember she shot herself," I say. "I just remember her death."

"It was awful," Mary says. "She was only there two weeks, and I guess she just couldn't take it." Mary keeps talking. Her voice is soothing. She is telling the story of her student's last days, wondering what that intelligent Smith grad had been thinking. She is saying war must be so horrible. I am remembering that Ed had a gun. I am remembering that day at the firing range. I am remembering I know just where the gun is. I am realizing I know how I can die.

When I get home, it is dark. I sit on the couch in my bathing suit and watch as Molly returns home from work, showers and leaves to go out. She asks if she can drive the Jeep, and I say no. That is Ed's car. She leaves, and I cry. I shout, "Ed where are you? Come home!" I think about the gun.

The gun is in our back hall, outside Ed's bathroom, in an old Army ammunition case. There is a lock on the case, and I don't have the key, but we have bolt cutters, and I know how to use them. I get the case. I put it on the coffee table. I think about the gun inside, how solid it felt in my hand when I fired it. I want to cut the lock. I want to touch the gun. I am scared. I call Mary.

"Hi Mary, it's me," I say. "Does Casey have a license to carry?" I think I sound perfectly rational.

"Why?"

"I'm thinking too much about Ed's gun, and I want it out of the house."

"He doesn't," she says. "But we could come get it."

I tell her no, it's against the law. I wonder out loud if it's even legal for me to have it, and she tells me to call the police and ask. "They'll know what to do," she says. And then she says, "Promise me you will call."

"I promise," I say.

I hang up and get the phone book. I want to call the business number, not 911. I don't want to create drama. I just want this gun out of the house. I search under "Easthampton, City of," but the police listing is not there. In the front of the book, I find listings for "Government," but "Police" isn't there either.

"Christ!" I shout. Finally I find it, under "Law Enforcement."

I call, and when the officer answers, I say, "My husband recently passed away. He had a gun, and a license to carry, but I don't, and the gun is here in the house. Is that legal?"

"No ma'am," the officer says. "I could send an officer to come pick it up."

I give him my address.

When I hang up, I put the case on the chest in the hall and sit back on the couch. I try not to stare at it. It is 9:15 p.m. Mary calls.

"Hi," she says. "Casey and I are on our way over. We have a DVD." She adds, "Did you call the police?"

I tell her they're on their way.

They aren't, though. I am so glad when Mary and Casey arrive. They sit with me in the living room, and we watch the clock together. It is 9:35. I could have unlocked the case and shot myself by now. Where are the cops? Casey is holding the DVD, a documentary on the Algerian revolution, and then there is a knock on the door, and I let the officer in. Tears start slipping down my face.

"I'm sorry for your loss, ma'am," he says, and he sounds like he means it. "Is this the gun?" He gestures toward the case, and I nod, hand it to him.

"Do you have the key?" he asks.

I shake my head, say, "No, but we have bolt cutters, and I know how to use them." I can see then he knows why I called, that it had nothing to do with licenses or legality. I sign a paper. I tell him I'm going to get a license to carry and when I do, I'll come pick it up. He says that would be fine, and he leaves. I run to the couch and fall into Mary's arms.

"Oh baby," she says. "It's good you did that."

"Ed loved that gun Mary," I say. "I should never have given it away."

I feel like I've lost another piece of him.

Mary and Casey offer to put in the DVD, and I am honest.

"I don't like documentaries, and I can't imagine watching a movie about Algeria," I say. I am laughing. "I'm okay now. What I'd really like to do is take a shower and go to bed."

I am smiling, and they don't seem offended, but Casey does say, "We like documentaries."

They leave, and after I shower I come back downstairs to watch a show. I keep looking at Ed's chair. It is so unthinkably strange that he is not in it.

At some point that night, I realize I stayed alive for a reason: I'm going to visit Ed's grandson Emmett in four days.

I'm walking on a dirt path through what appears to be a lush garden, and I see Ed in front of me. There are people around him, sitting on benches and large slabs of granite and Goshen stone. Ed is entertaining a crowd.

I hurry closer. My heart lifts at the sight of him. His thick gray curls, his broad shoulders, his wire-framed glasses perched on his nose.

Ed is telling a joke, a Seinfeld joke about pharmacists that always cracked him up.

"Why do they get to wear lab coats and stand up high on a podium, like they're better than us?" Ed says.

He tells other jokes, then he steps away from his podium and walks down a grassy slope that leads into heavy cover. I follow him.

"Ed," I call to him. "I found you. And you were so funny."

"Nobody knows those jokes here," he says, hugging me. "They think I'm funny."

He is laughing, at ease.

"Come home with me," I say.

"I can't," he says. "I don't want to. It's good for me here. I feel good. I've never felt this good."

The sound of my own sobbing wakes me. But the dream makes sense. Ed is happy, and I am glad for him.

A few days later, I lie in bed and consciously go back to the meadow where I found Ed in my dream. He is there, on a narrow grassy path bordered on both sides by a gradual slope. His back is to me, and he is walking.

"Ed! Ed!" I holler.

I am restful but not sleepy, conscious that I am driving this vision. My eyes are closed. I catch up to Ed, and he turns around. He is so happy to see me.

"Will you please come home with me?"

"Janice," he says. "I can't."

He takes my hands in his, and he looks into my eyes, and I want him.

"Can we lie together then?" I ask.

"Sure."

We walk until we find a flat grassy area. Ed lies down on his back, and I lie on top of him. I smell his scent — a combination of shampoo, sawdust and incense. I rest my head on his shoulder.

"I love you," I tell him.

"I love you, too," he says.

I fall asleep.

Chapter Nine

Ry got a promotion around the time Ed died, and he has a new work schedule that conflicts with Kisha's medical assistant internship at a physician's office. They have asked me to babysit Emmett on Wednesday. I don't see Emmett as often as I see Eli, so I am eager for the chance to spend time with him.

Before I leave I have breakfast with my friend Ericka, a colleague from Cooley Dickinson Hospital. She tells me she is interviewing for a new job at UMass, and I am relieved for her.

I don't complain about my boss or the loss of my job. I love my boss, and I don't feel angry at anyone. Just scared.

When I arrive at Kisha and Ry's apartment in Beverly, Massachusetts, a two-hour drive from my home, Emmett is in day care. I give Ry a picture of Ed patting Emmett's curls on one of those last days he was alive. Ry loves the picture, and he puts it on the fridge.

We do errands, and then we drive to the YMCA in Beverly to get Emmett. Back in their home, he has time to relax into knowing me again before his parents have to leave. I study Emmett's face, and I can see Ed in him. I love to watch how he moves, what he does.

When Ry and Kisha leave, Emmett doesn't cry. We play with trucks on the floor, then head for the beach.

I take an Ativan before we leave. Just in case. I notice it doesn't dissolve in my mouth like it usually does. Only for an instant, I wonder why.

Emmett is settled in his carriage, content and quiet. I am lost in thought, talking to Ed.

"I'm with Emmett, honey. We're going to the beach." I feel so together. I am out of bed. I am moving, and I am not thinking about ways to die.

At the beach, Emmett sits in the sand with me. It is still September, and it's unseasonably warm. We pile sand on each other's feet. We use mussel shells as if they were shovels. We play with large stones. Emmett is so lovely, I think to myself.

The last time I was at this beach I was with Ed. He had on his Life Is Good T-shirt, and he had Emmett on his back. Emmett was about six months old. A picture from that day is on the wall in my bedroom.

Kisha asked me to feed Emmett his dinner at 5:30, and when I check my phone for the time, it is already 5:15. I don't want to leave, and Emmett doesn't either. I am afraid of the transition. I don't want him to be unhappy, so we keep sitting there. Then, Emmett stands up and gestures for me to pick him up. We walk to the shore and I look up at the horizon. All I can see is the background that's behind Ed in the photo in my room, and I start to weep quietly. Emmett puts his two little arms around me and holds me tight. It feels like Ed is holding me instead of a child, and I'm convinced Ed is comforting me through this sweet child.

I walk Emmett to the stroller and buckle him in.

Emmett says, "Ball."

I look up and see a beach ball, right where we were sitting.

"Yes, Emmett. Ball," I say.

Then I notice what the ball says: "Life Is Good." Just like Ed's shirt.

"Emmett, your Grampa *is* here. I knew it." All the way back to Ry's house I think to myself, "If Ed keeps finding me, I can do this."

I give Emmett his dinner, and then a sponge bath before putting him to bed. I feel like I've completed an important project, and I am excited I get to spend tomorrow with Emmett as well. I shower to get the sand off of me, and put on a pair of Ed's boxer shorts and a mustard-colored T-shirt. I still have to make the 20-minute drive to Judy's, where I'm spending the night, but I'm sure no one will see me in this odd outfit. I swallow another Ativan and lie on the couch to read. It is 6:30, and Kisha won't be home for three hours.

I read for a while, then get antsy. I stand up and stretch, do yoga. I walk around. I make tea. I look at the photos on my cell phone. There are so many of Ed that go back eight years, and I have only just noticed them. I study them all, and I cry and cry. It is only 7:45.

By 8:30, I am agitated, weepy. I text Molly, telling her I am lonely. I text Judy, telling her I might not be hungry when I arrive. I can't wait to be snug in her house.

The next hour creeps by, and when Kisha comes in, I tell her how much I enjoyed being with Emmett. We hug, and I leave.

I reach for the GPS in my glove compartment and realize it's not there. Suddenly, I am flooded in panic.

I dial Judy.

"Oh my God," I say. "I think I'm going to have a nervous breakdown."

"What's up, Buggy?"

"I don't know how to get to where you are. I don't have my GPS."

Judy asks if I can go inside and use Ry's computer to go on Mapquest, and I say, no. No, I can't do it. Judy doesn't understand why, and frankly, neither do I. My legs are shaking. I want to start driving, but I don't even know which way to turn at the end of their road. Judy is calming, says she'll go online to get directions and will call me back. I sit there, waiting.

"Okay Bug," she says. She is chipper. I need this. She directs me to Route 128 and tells me to call when I near the exit for Route 1. I hang up and start driving. Things feel okay until I'm on the highway. There is so much traffic. So many red tail lights. I am terrified. I am only going 60 miles an hour, but it feels like 90. I am holding on to the steering wheel so tightly my hands hurt.

To die is what I have longed for for 10 days, and now, suddenly, threatened by accidental death, what I want is my life. I think about Molly, about how it would be for her if she was awakened by the police in the night to learn her mother was killed in an accident near Boston. What would happen to Sally? To Eli? They need me. I have to be strong.

I turn off the radio. The trip seems endless. I am still on 128. There is no sign for Route 1. Where is it? I want to call Judy, but I need both hands on the wheel. Good Christ, this is not me. I love to drive. I can drive anywhere, any time. Ed hated driving, traveling, and I become convinced I have taken on his anxieties.

My heart is beating so hard it hurts, and I am sweating. I want to open the window, but I can't let go of the wheel. There are cars in front of me, beside me, behind me. There are police on the side of the road. I want them to stop me. I want to call 911. But I am wearing only my dead husband's underwear, and I have his T-shirt on and no bra. No one can see me like this. I can't call for help.

"You can do this Janice. You can do this." I am talking out loud. Then I see Route 1. I get off and call Judy. My hands are shaking so hard it is an effort to hold onto the phone. She gives me the next set of directions, and tells me to call when I get off at her exit.

I have never been this agitated before. I think I am having a heart attack. Panic rushes through me and I take huge gulping breaths. I open the window. I close it. The wind is too loud. I can't think.

At the exit, I call Judy. "Am I getting close?" I say. "I am freaking out, Jude."

She tells me to turn, and I turn. She tells me to go through two lights, and I do. She tells me to take a right and says it's her street. She tells me to look for her.

"I can't see you." I am screeching into the phone. Then she is waving to me. She looks so tired. I pull over and as soon as my car stops, I start to scream.

"Edddddddddd. Oh my God. Ahhhhhhh. Oh my God." It is so loud in my car. I am making all this noise. The windows grab the sound and hold it in. I am shaking and so is my car.

"I don't want to die," I scream, loud. I yell it over and over. I am the porcelain woman on my windowsill now. I am on a ledge. Then, all of a sudden I can see. There are people on the sidewalk. I am in the city.

"OK, Bug," I say. "Time to normalize."

Judy has run into the house to get the on-street parking pass, and when she comes out I put her hand on my heart.

"Feel this."

"Oh my God," she says. "Let me take your bag."

But I won't let her. There is not much I can do for myself right now, but I can hold the damn bag.

My heart is still racing when we sit down. I take two more Ativan — four milligrams — and I can't wait for it to kick in. Judy and I talk for a while, and then she goes to bed. I can see on her face how stressed out she is by her job. I tell her, "Judy, quit your job and come work with me. We'll revive Beetle Press."

She says, "Yeah. Goodnight, Buggy."

I try to read in the living room, but I can't concentrate. Now I have diarrhea, and I keep running to the bathroom. Her apartment is tiny: one bedroom, one bathroom, a kitchenette and living room. At 1 a.m., she calls into the bathroom.

"Are you okay, Bug?" she asks me.

"I can't sleep. I'm sorry. I'll be quiet."

I go back to the couch. I am very angry at the pharmacist because this Ativan is not working. I think it was mislabeled. I think maybe I need to be in the hospital. I think about Ed. He is dead, I think. Yes, I'm sure of it. He is dead. I wonder if Judy knows. I don't think she does. I have to fight myself to not wake her up. She has finally fallen asleep, but I need to tell her that Ed is gone. I don't think she knows. I can't remember. I want to tell her. I want her to know. I want my mother. I turn the light on and sit up.

I pick up the pill bottle. I am thinking about taking another Ativan — the generic version is what I have, Lorazapam. I think I need another. I take one, pop it in my mouth and swallow. I'm thinking about finding a CVS tomorrow before I head back to Ry's to babysit to find out what is in here. It is not Ativan, not Lorazapam, it can't be, because it is not working. I study the bottle. It says "Lexapro" on the label. That's the antidepressant I have been taking on and off for almost 16 years. Ten milligrams a day. I calculate what I have taken today and realize I've had 100 milligrams of Lexapro and no Ativan.

"You asshole," I say. I am laughing. I feel so relieved. I thought I was going crazy, but I am taking the wrong Goddamned drug. I wonder for a minute if I should make myself throw up, if I have overdosed, but I really don't care. I want to sleep, and I now know I don't have the Ativan that will make that happen. But I do have Ambien.

I find my Ambien and take two instead of one because I am so very tired. It is 2:30 in the morning, and I just want to fall asleep. I think about my breakfast with Ericka. It was so long ago. Days. Or was it just this morning?

I am fucked up. I am in and out of the bathroom. I can't fall asleep. I am terrified at the thought of driving home tomorrow. I think I will call my brother Jeff in the morning and ask him to come get me at Ry's after I babysit. This seems like a reasonable solution. I curl up in a ball. I feel better already. I put my thumb in my mouth and suck it, something I haven't done since I was 12. I fall asleep.

I wake up at ten of 7 like I've set an alarm, and I move into Judy's room. I know she will start work at 7, and her living room is her office. I crawl in her bed and fall asleep. I don't hear her get up, and I don't hear the clacking of her keyboard until 10:30 a.m. Immediately, I need the bathroom. I am shaking so hard I can hardly get my pajama pants down. I am panicked because I remember I have to be back in Beverly at noon, and I can't breathe with the fright. I can't drive back there. I can't.

I am wet and sweaty. I collapse back in Judy's bed and try to think, but instead, I cry. I remember my plan to call Jeff, and I know what I need to do. I will ask him to come babysit with me and then drive me home. I don't know how I will get to Beverly. I hope Jeff will help me figure that out.

My phone is shaking in my hand, and I can't read the names in my contact list. Judy is on the phone with someone in the other room. She sounds so professional, and I am struggling to figure out how to make my phone work. Finally I hit my brother's name, and I hear dialing. His wife, Wendy, answers.

"Jan," she says. "How are you?" She hears me crying. "Oh, not very good. What's going on?"

Words spill out. "I need to babysit in Beverly. I need a ride. Can you come help me?" Something like that.

"Jan, where are you?" she asks me.

I try to tell her what is going on. She asks if someone is with me, and I tell her Judy, but she is working, and I don't want to bother her.

She says, "Jan, you need help."

I ask her again if she will come take me to Beverly and help me babysit Emmett.

"Jan," she says. "You can't babysit."

"I have to," I tell her. I am still thinking that my problem is travel anxieties, and that Ed never let that get in his way, even when he was suffering. "Ed wouldn't want me to disappoint Riley."

"Jan." She keeps repeating my name. I can tell this means she is serious. "It wouldn't be safe for you to take care of Emmett. You need to call Riley."

Judy comes in the room. She is talking to me. Wendy is talking to me. I don't know what to do. I hand Judy my phone. I can't imagine why this is happening. I don't know who I am, why I'm so fucked up. I was normal before. Before, at the beach and with Emmett. I want to see him again. Why won't somebody take me?

Judy hangs up and tells me someone will come get me. Two people have to come, from Gilford, N.H., to Somerville to pick me up, drive me and my car to Easthampton, and then go back home. I am mortified. I am altering everyone's day. I hate myself.

Then I call Riley. I don't know what I say to him, but when we hang up, he knows I can't come. I should feel relieved, but I don't. Before Ed died, I was afraid I would lose his children, and I am sure this is the moment it is starting. It is the moment I will lose everything. Molly, Sally, Eli. I will lose them if I can't take care of myself. I want to go home. I want to know who is coming and when. I want to go home now.

It is an effort to shower. I do it because I smell. Then I pace up and down Judy's hallway. I know this must be annoying, so I go outside. My brother Allan calls me. He is coming with Wendy because Jeff is at work. I thank him. I tell him I'm sorry. I ask when he's leaving. I ask him if he will help me figure out if I should be admitted to the hospital.

I go inside. I pack my bags. I pace some more. Judy has a teleconference at noon, so I leave again. I am so in the way. It is nice out, and the breeze feels so good on my face. I sit on the stoop of the apartment building, like a city person. I call Allan and talk at him while he drives.

"Can I tell you two things, Allan?"

"Sure."

"I learned something last night. In the car. When I was driving here from Riley's. I learned I don't want to die." I am crying again. I am manic.

"That's good," Allan says, then after a moment of silence, "Jannie, didn't you have a second thing to tell me?"

"I do," I say. I am glad he reminded me. "I sucked my thumb last night to fall asleep."

He laughs.

"Al, please don't tell mom and dad you have to come get me. They would be scared. I am scared, Al." He is laughing again. I think he has already told them. Maybe they are coming too. They will not know me. "Did you tell them?" I am very paranoid.

He says he did not.

I have to let Al go because he is driving, but I don't want to hang up. It feels good to be talking.

I call Melissa and leave her a message. I call the school psychiatrist, whom I know well. I leave her a message, too, tell her I might need her to prepare Molly that I'm going to be hospitalized. I want to go in the hospital. I want to be sedated. I want to sleep and sleep and not think anymore. But I want to be home. I want to lie in my bed and look at Ed on the wall and talk to him.

I rock on the stoop. I cry. I hold my head in my hands. Ed would not know who I am.

I call Bonni, and she talks to me for over an hour. I tell her the same two things I told Allan. It's like confession. When I tell her I sucked my thumb, she asks me, "Did it help?"

"Yes," I say, and I cry. I think that was such a good question.

"Bonni, I need help. I'm falling apart, and I don't know how to do it because I've never fallen apart before."

"No, you haven't, Janice. You are the strongest person I know."

I'm sure she is relieved when I tell her my therapist is calling and that I have to go. I am sitting in my car now and have rolled down the windows. I don't care who hears me. I am so fucking sad. I am so scared. I want to go home. It is 12:20 now.

I tell Melissa about the drugs I mixed up, and I tell her about taking the Ambien.

"I'm not sure that was a good idea," she says, but it is kind, not a criticism.

I am crying so hard I can't speak, but then words come out. "Remember Ed had travel anxieties? It is awful, Melissa. I didn't know how awful it was. And you know what I think is happening to me? I think I have taken on Ed's anxieties. I think he gave them to me. Will I feel like this always?"

"No, Janice. That is not happening. That does *not* happen to people." She sounds so sure, and I want to believe it. "Ed loved you. He wouldn't want you to feel this way. You don't have to take on his anxieties. He doesn't want you to. I know that.

"Are you sure?"

"That does *not* happen to people." I'm glad she has repeated it.

"Then what is happening to me?"

"Your body is suffering from chemical warfare. You will feel better, maybe even tomorrow."

"Can I take Ativan when I get home?"

"I don't think that's a good idea. I think your body should rest."

I ask her again, and she says, "Maybe you should think about calling your doctor." Melissa always says you should think about doing something when she thinks that's what you should do.

I know she is right, but I say, "I'm afraid to call her. I'm afraid she'll be mad at me."

I think about being in the hospital again, and now I don't want to be there. Melissa has made me feel like I'm going to be okay. I try to ask her if she will tell Allan I don't have to go to the hospital, but what comes out is this: "If if if if if if if."

Soon, Al is calling. "Sista," he says. "Where are you? I am parked in front of the address you gave me."

I look around. I don't see him. But then there he is at the top of the hill. He's going to take me home. He is walking down the hill toward me. I jump out of my car and run to him. I reach him, and I hold him so tightly.

"Wow," he says. "That's the best hug I ever got from you."

We walk with our arms around each other's waist. His waist doesn't feel like Ed's, but it feels really good.

Then I see Wendy, and I hug her too. I don't want to let go. I am so grateful.

I text Judy, and she comes out to get us. We use her bathroom. I notice that the toilet paper has run out, and because refreshing paper is something I know how to do, I think I should change it.

My hands are shaking. I don't think I'll be able to do it. But I peel off the old tube, and trembling, pull a new one from the rack on the floor. I slip it on the metal bar and it clacks with my unsteadiness. I hear it snap in place. I have contributed something.

In the car, I am severely agitated and feel sorry for Al, having to spend his entire day taking me home. I am useless. I tell Al that I've put in a claim on Ed's life insurance but that I'm afraid they won't pay it, and that will be the complete undoing of me.

"No it won't," he tells me, and I decide to trust in that.

Every 10 minutes or so, I ask Al, "Do you hear sirens?" He doesn't. To me, they are so loud. My face itches, and I scratch and scratch. He peers at me, "You're a mess, Sista."

I stare out the window. The trees are bare, and I realize I don't know what month it is or when Ed died. I think about it. I look hard for clues, but then I have to give in.

"Al," I say. "What season is it? I mean, I know it's not winter or summer, but is it spring or fall?"

"It's fall, Sista," he says. "It's the end of September."

Right. September. That's when Ed died. I realize I will not be able to take care of Molly, or even myself, when I get home, and I call Mary.

"Mary," I say. "It's a long story, but my brother is driving me back from Boston, and I want him to be able to leave to drive home when we get there, but I don't think I should be alone. Do you think you could come over?"

"Oh Jan, sure I could," she says. "I love that you're asking for help."

I start crying again. Then I laugh. "It's a good thing I have a lot of friends, because I'm using them up."

Al asks me about Ed's death, and I describe it in painful detail. It is the only thing on this day that I am clear about.

My phone rings. It is the guy who repaired the crumbling bench seat in my boat. He wants me to pick it up tomorrow, and I tell him I will be there before noon. While I'm talking, Al is miming to me, whispering, "No plans for tomorrow, Jannie. Don't make any plans."

I ignore him. When I hang up, I write, "Noon. Boat guy," in enormous letters on a letter-sized piece of paper and place it on the dashboard.

When we're almost home, I get a text from Judy: "Bug, I can see you changed the toilet paper." For a moment I'm so proud of myself. Then I read the rest: "You put it on upside down. Given the day you're having, I'll let it slide."

I smile.

We turn onto my street. Wendy, who's been driving the second car, pulls in the driveway behind us, and we walk to my back door. I feel Ed. We stand there for a minute until I realize I am the one with the key. I run back to the car and pull a set of keys from the console. I try them in the lock, one by one.

"Sorry," I say. "I've never used these. Ed was always home when I got here."

"Ed, which key is it, honey?" I ask. Then the knob turns in my hand, and we are inside.

My heart is slamming so hard in my chest that I can't sit down. I bring in the mail. Carry my suitcase to the bottom of the stairs. Peer inside the refrigerator even though I'm not hungry. I offer food to Al and Wendy. It is about 4:30, and I know they want to head home.

We sit and talk about Ed, about our visit to New Hampshire and those nice summer days on the lake, and then Mary arrives. She flops down on the couch next to me.

"Baby," she says. "What have you done to yourself?"

I tell her the story, keeping the tiresome tale short since I've told it so much today.

She chooses her words carefully. "I don't know a lot about medicine, but don't you think you should call your doctor?"

Someone has said it. We all know a doctor will make me go to the hospital, and we all know I don't want to go. Mary is making a tactical move.

"I don't want to call my doctor. I'm afraid she'll be mad at me," I say. Finally, after more nudging from Al and Wendy, I agree that Mary can call Dr. Baker, but I don't want to talk to her.

After Al and Wendy leave, Mary calls the doctor and leaves a message. I walk from the kitchen to the dining room to the hall and back to the kitchen, round and round and round. We eat macaroni and cheese that Ed's mother made, and my doctor calls Mary back. I hear Mary explain the situation as I walk and walk some more. Husband died. Took 100 milligrams of Lexapro. Meant to take Ativan. Wasn't an overdose.

"I didn't mean to do this," I yell from the living room into the kitchen. "It was an accident."

Mary repeats that to the doctor, for my benefit.

"How do you feel right now?" Mary asks me, but I know she knows the answer.

I am honest. "Like I'm having a heart attack."

Mary hangs up and tells me the doctor wants me to go to the emergency room. Once again, I start to cry. "I don't want to go to the hospital. I just got home. I want to be home."

"Jan." Over and over today, people are saying my name like I am a small child. "You need to find out if there's any damage. You took a lot of medication."

"But I can't go to Cooley Dickinson. I just lost my job there. And what about Molly? I don't want her to be scared."

"If Molly sees you now, she will be scared."

74

In the hospital parking lot, I start to quake. "I can't go in there Mary. I can't do it." But her arm is around me, and we are walking toward the Emergency Department door.

At the triage desk, I bury my head in her chest. "Please Mary don't make me do this I don't want to be here I don't want to be here I don't want to do this." The doors to the treatment rooms open, and Mary guides me in. I have been in this place countless times, and I have never seen anyone not in an ambulance get inside that fast.

The triage nurse is on hold with poison control, and she's asking me so many questions. Simple questions, like what is my name? My date of birth? I think very hard.

Suddenly, I wonder how long it's been since Ed's been gone. I think it's been months, and I ask Mary, but she won't give me an answer. She says she doesn't know. Then I am sobbing, "Mary, please tell me when Ed died. How long has he been gone?"

When Mary tells me it's been just over two weeks, I start to keen, and the triage nurse becomes nervous.

"Can you believe I'm still on hold," she says, patting my hand.

"I'm so sorry," I tell her. "I am usually normal."

In the treatment room, they can't get my blood to flow into a tube. Mary is crying. My feet are jiggling at the end of the bed. I am hooked up to an EKG, and a line is squiggling on a piece of paper. It looks crazy, like one of Eli's drawings instead of the well-known pattern for heart rhythm. The nurse asks me to keep still, and I do it, but it is a tremendous effort. I have to think about it, hard.

A man comes in to take my insurance information. He asks me if I am married or single.

"I don't know," I sob. "Mary, what am I?"

Mary explains to him that I just lost my husband, and when I can't remember my address, she gives it to him. He asks for my phone number. Slowly, the numbers come to me, and I say them out loud.

"Why is this so fucking hard?" I shout. "Why can't I remember? Did I damage my brain? Will I be like this always?" I am frightened.

The man asks about my employer, then, studying the information in his tablet computer, he realizes I once worked where he does. He tries to move on, but I don't let him.

"I worked here, until I was eliminated. I was eliminated, and then my husband was eliminated." I can't make myself stop talking.

"Mary," I say. "Can you call Molly and tell her what is going on? She must be worried."

"Jan," Mary says. "She would be very worried if she heard you. And we don't know what's going on." Mary's voice is so smooth and controlled. I remember I used to be like that.

"But she has school tomorrow, and there's nobody home."

"I'll call her soon," Mary says.

"And Sally too?" I ask.

"Yes, and Sally too."

A nurse gives me two milligrams of Ativan and leaves the room.

When a doctor finally appears, he asks what brought me here, and I talk for what seems like 15 minutes, and then realize he didn't need to hear most of what I said. I'm talking about driving on the highway in Ed's underwear and no bra. Things like that. In my ridiculousness, though, somehow I feel safe. I know this doctor. He is not judging me. I can tell.

He asks me what I want. "I want to sleep," I say. "I want Ativan right in my vein. A lot of it, and then I want to go home and sleep."

"We can do that," he says.

Mary drives me home and calls Molly and Sally. I go to bed and sleep and sleep, and Mary sleeps over and takes care of Molly and buys groceries for me in the morning, and her husband, Casey, picks up the boat seat at noon. I sleep and Mary makes Jell-O.

Chapter Ten

L ying in bed one Thursday well past Noon, I can't find one good reason to compel me out of the sheets. I talk to Ed on the wall. "What should I do, honey?" He smiles back, oblivious to how alone he has left me.

I finally make laundry and errands my goal for the day, and I am up. As I move about the house, I remember the DVD that Bonni and her family made of the day Ed and I got married.

Once I remember the DVD is in the house, finding it is all I can focus on. I look in the box where we keep memorabilia. My two brothers, lauded as "Gilford Entrepreneurs" in a New Hampshire newspaper headline, smile up at me, but there is no DVD.

I run to the television cabinet and sort through all the DVDs. I am crying now. "It's gone. Where could it be?" I search with my hand, far back in the cabinet. "Ed and Jan's Wedding Vows." I have it. Now, I am afraid to watch it. So I plan the rest of my day around it.

I go to the bank, return a friend's pie dish, buy paint thinner, go to CVS for my prescriptions. Then I buy a tea and a sandwich and go to one of our favorite places — the field where the three horses roam. Today, there are dozens of grackles swooping about, taking turns having a bath in a shallow puddle. I watch them for a very long time, stalling.

When I finally get the DVD started, the laptop's battery dies, and I have to put everything away and head home. I lie in a patch of sun on the grass for a half hour. I use the paint thinner to remove glue patches from a canister lid I repaired. I fold the last load of laundry. Then I settle on the couch with a full box of tissues, and I turn the DVD on.

I watch it straight through, weeping at the familiar scenes and full-out wailing when I see clips of Ed, when he speaks, when he calls me by name.

We made the DVD in the weeks before the wedding so we did not have to exchange our vows live; Ed was nervous about that.

I love remembering how we picked the DVD's background scenes: our yard, the field and river where we took Angus to play while we had tea, the tower in Greenfield where Ed asked me to marry him. He had invited me up there on a chilly, drizzly day for tea and finally had to point out the message he'd written on the tower's top, in red Sharpie: "I love you J. Will you marry me?"

I rewind that section over and over. The Sharpie, even then, had already started to run in the rain and was now probably long gone. Too much of Ed is fading away.

The next section is the exchange of our vows. I tell Ed how much I love him and why. I promise to always be his soul mate, and we kiss. Then it is Ed's turn. He looks so uncomfortable, nervous. He didn't like making this video; he did it for me.

I lean on his left shoulder. His hair is long — before he cut it for the ceremony — and the thick silver waves curl back away from his face. He is a few days away from a shave, and I love the thick scruff. I reach out to touch it.

I almost cannot bear to look at him. He is so beautiful. I had forgotten how strong and masculine he was before the cancer.

I look at his favorite chair just to make sure he is not sitting there, watching me. Then I turn behind me and see his urn.

As I listen to his vows, I yell at the computer screen.

"Janice, you, too, are my soul mate and best friend, and I love you with all my heart. You took me, a broken man, and seeing something in me, nurtured me back to mental and physical health."

I need you now, Ed. I am broken, and only you can fix me.

"I'm a better and stronger man because of your love. You are always mindful of my individual needs, most especially the connection with my sons."

Ed, Ed, you are so beautiful. Please come back. I can't do this without you. Please…

"Very important to me is that I trust you implicitly in every part of our life. I think of you as my lifelong partner, able to deal with whatever is cast our way.

I can't deal with it, Ed.

"… using our similarities and differences to show us the way, I the turtle and you the hare." Ed smiles when he says this. He likes his little joke. Ed was a patient, methodical man. I am impulsive, hurried. What I notice though isn't the joke; it's Ed's smile. How I miss that smile.

"Sometimes just simply sitting and talking with you is a fulfilling journey. I look forward to the next chapters — marriage and being grandparents — with great enthusiasm. I love you."

I love you too, Ed, but no one told us about this chapter.

I watch the video several more times. The end shot shows our mailbox tag: "Godleski, Beetle, Scaife," representing Ed, me, the girls.

I'm so sad I can't breathe.

Chapter Eleven

I remember the old television ad that showed an egg, whole in its shell. The voice-over said, "This is your brain." Then a hand cracked the egg into a hot frying pan, and the albumen began to sizzle. Voice-over: "This is your brain on drugs."

Crack the egg, beat it, hard, until it froths. Scramble it. Run it through your disposal. Look to see if it's still there. Often.

This is your brain on grief.

I start going through Ed's belongings, starting with his desk. I find several pocket watches and a jar of coins. There are kids' report cards and newspaper clippings, like one about Lee and his friend playing sax on the street in Amherst to make money.

And I find the letters I wrote to Ed every year for his birthday. On his 48th birthday, I wrote down 48 things I loved about him. On the 49th, there were 49, and so on. I read the letter from his 50th birthday: You work on a problem until it's solved; You talk to me and tell stories; You even talk in your sleep; You listen as well as you talk, and you always have good advice; You snuggle; Your eyes captivate me;

Your body is a rock; Even simple things make you happy.

I see Ed's notebook, in which he jotted to-do lists and thoughts for songs. I thumb through to the last page, and I see the beginning of the song I had asked for so many times. The handwriting is shaky, uneven, and this tells me that Ed was writing while he was on morphine, but the words are clear:

I've tried to write this song before

Tried so many times

But all I ever seem to write is

Dark and …

That's the end. I close his desk. I will organize his things another day.

When I tell Sally about Clif, the appliance repairman, she tells me that Tommy, Eli's father and her live-in boyfriend once again, could fix my dishwasher. I did not know that he could, or that he would. She tells me Tommy could manage the other tasks I have worried about, too.

I am so very desperate that I call Tommy, and he is nice. "Sure. I can do that," he tells me. It is like we never have argued, which, of course, we have.

We agree I will pay him $10 an hour. He fixes the dishwasher, mounting it solidly to the floor so that it closes. He helps hold a mammoth tag sale; I give the money to Hospice and the Cancer Connection. He paints the chapel and the garage, bringing in his friend, Tito. I enjoy their company.

"You shouldn't go to Florida," I tell him. He has been talking about moving there. "Eli needs you. … I need you." I laugh. He does too.

Driving Tommy home that day, I half listen as he tells me about a new PlayStation game he has. Then a man with a generous head of gray hair drives by in a green Rav4, and I think it's Ed. I turn to follow him. Then I realize Tommy is in the car.

If Tommy hadn't been with me, I would have followed that man home.

One day I remember the photos I found on my phone when I was taking care of Emmett. I have to get them out. I load them onto a data card and drive to CVS.

On the screen of the photo machine, the images take on life. There are my brothers one Thanksgiving; there is Angus after a trip to the groomer; there are Sally and Molly on the Ohio River. Then there is Ed, in my living room at North Maple, and I am crying. I race through more photos, until I find Ed again.

There he is, lying with me on the couch, having a date. There he is again, standing next to the Mill River in Florence, wearing his jeans and black hooded sweatshirt; his stomach is swollen, so this must be when his liver was failing. And there he is, squatting near the Manhan River, throwing sticks for Angus.

Then I see Ed on his birthday, cards all over his lap, and a bow on his head that I stuck there so I could send a photo text to Lee to remind him to call his dad and wish him a happy birthday.

Ed was 55 in that picture, the oldest he will ever be.

Finally there is Ed when he was so sick he was dying, on our sofa, clutching the comforter that Judy gave him.

The photos fall out of the machine, and I sort them into two piles: Ed and not Ed.

When I get home, I put the photos of Ed in order, like a little flip book. I don't include the very last photo, when he was sick on the couch. I put double-sided tape on that one and attach it to my nightstand.

That photo is a comfort. I bring a Maglite to bed with me each night, and I fall asleep talking to Ed, just like I always did. This photo, of all the photos of Ed around the house, is a particular comfort to me. Why this one, I wonder? And then it comes to me. This Ed, of all the Eds, is not wearing his glasses. I can see his eyes, his beautiful blue eyes. And they can see me, too.

Chapter Twelve

I am a seeker of widows. I want to know what they know.

My dear friend Molly Robinson, my Molly's godmother, calls me daily and listens to my wails and moans. She talks to me patiently about how the hurt will settle, how it won't feel so bad in time.

Molly, who lost her first husband, Tom, is remarried to Don Robinson, and I ask her how she could ever love again. She talks to me about this, too. How it is possible. How it takes time.

I need to hear over and over that someday I will feel better. So one day, I turn to Judy's mother, Bette Kelliher, who lives at Providence Place, a gorgeous retirement home founded by the Sisters of Providence.

Bette was widowed twice and has more children and grandchildren than you could count. At 88, she is amusing, full of life. I need to hear how she does it. How she keeps living after losing love twice.

"My teeny-tiny Bug person," she says in a screechy falsetto as she greets me, as she always does.

Over lunch, Bette tells me the details of losing her first husband, who died in France during the war and left her with an infant son. She tells me about losing her second husband, Bob, and how she kept right on because she had eight children to care for, even though they were grown. She tells me other stories, and then we move on to lighter topics.

On my way out, I visit the chapel to pray. I have not felt the hands of God on my shoulder since that day in May when I followed the school bus. I am in a cave; I can feel only myself, and every now and again, I feel Ed.

In the elevator, an idea comes to me. I could teach writing to senior citizens – people who have stories to tell.

I find the activities director and pitch my idea to her.

"I have been looking for you for two years," Sister Joan tells me.

The first class is two weeks later. To start it, I ask the group — five women, including Bette, and one man, Leo — to write a brief story that would show me who they are.

I participate, and this is part of what I write:

The young voice on the answering machine said, "This is the voice mail for Roger Malo, the electrician. Please leave a message."

I needed a new ceiling fan installed in my bathroom, and since my handy husband has left me for heaven, I do need to leave Roger a message. I know Roger, and he knows my circumstances, so I say, "This is Janice, the unemployed widow. Please return my call."

I am in my new office. My bed. Since being laid off from my job at Cooley Dickinson Hospital and watching my husband die four days later, it is the safest place from which to do business.

They each read their stories, and they are fabulous. Bette writes about her satin button-up underwear falling down at a dance when she was 13. Leo doesn't read what he has written because he can't decipher his handwriting. He tells us stories instead, and I have to interrupt him several times to get him back on track. I read my piece, and I know they understand what it's like to feel adrift. It scares me that I identify with them.

During our second writing exercise, one of the women tells a tale that makes me roar with laughter, though there is nothing funny about it except the adept way she has written it. As a child, she was able to discern that her father was having an affair with his secretary, who lived right down the street. When the secretary became ill, her unknowing mother made her deliver chicken soup to the mistress. This grown woman, then a young teen, did so only after a battle. She wrote that she handed over the soup and blurted, "You son of a bitch" before running away.

I loved the energy in the room, and that I would get to hear more of their stories.

But back home in the driveway, any good feeling I'd had disappeared. I couldn't bear to go inside my empty house. I sat in the warm car for over an hour and looked out at the rain falling down, collecting like tears on the windshield. When Molly got home, I followed her inside, pretending that I'd just arrived, too. It was safe in there now.

To get to sleep last night I took my usual two milligrams of Ativan and a shot of Nyquil, but I added Trazadone, a sleeping pill, to the cocktail because I have been so tired and just cannot sleep. Still, I tossed and turned, my mouth pasty and dry, my tongue sticking to my palate.

I wake at 6:36 a.m. to get Molly off to school, though really all I do now for her is simply make sure she is awake and moving, tentatively calling, "Molly, time to go." I am just a whisper in the world.

I step out of bed and take six steps toward the bathroom when my head fills with light. I am falling. When I am conscious again, I am on my back in the hallway outside Molly's room. Something is very wrong.

Molly slides open her door. She finds her naked mother on the floor.

"Mom, what are you doing?" she asks. She is still full of worry for me, sure that without Ed, I will die too.

"I felt dizzy."

"Are we going to Emmanuel College today?"

"Sure," I say from my prone position. "Yes."

I am thinking about how I will make that happen.

I make my way back to bed and tell Molly I will contact the school for the tour times. At 9, she sends me a text message to say that Emmanuel's tour begins at 2 p.m. I text back that I will be ready to leave at 11:30. At 11, I get up and I sit in the shower because I know I will fall if I stand.

I am a worthless mother. My daughter, who has survived divorce and death, just wants to choose a college. I have to help her.

I'm steady when Molly comes home from school, and we head for Emmanuel, in Boston. I sneak off to the bathroom while Molly is filling out paperwork and pop two milligrams of Ativan in my mouth. I want to make this experience pleasant. No crying.

The tour takes us across the small campus, through the dining hall, a dormitory, an academic building. There are two snappy guides who take turns walking backward and three parent-child sets.

Forty-five minutes into the tour, I can see Molly is thinking about how she might get along on this city campus. She listens as the guides talk about the course load, study abroad. Inside the fitness center, they talk about using the equipment whenever they want. Suddenly, I am dizzy. I was in the front of the group with Molly, holding doors for the other parents, and now I am lagging behind. I stumble, then fall to the ground and scramble up.

"Are you okay, mom?"

"I'm fine," I tell Molly.

I take two more steps, and I plunge. My head hits the tiled wall on the right side, but I keep walking. I am afraid we are losing the group. The parents and teenagers and the perky guides have turned a corner.

"Mom!" Molly says. She has heard my head hit the wall, or seen it. She must also see I am stumbling.

"I don't want to lose the group," I say.

"Mom. You can't walk," Molly says.

The last things I hear are the thud of my head hitting the floor and Molly's cry: "Mom!"

When I open my eyes, a large, muscular man is kneeling next to me. "Don't sit up just yet," he says. "Are you okay?"

"My husband died." That's what comes out.

"Yes, your daughter said you've been having a hard time."

"I wanted to give her a normal day," I say to the man. "I was trying…"

He cuts me off. "It's okay," he says.

There is amazing kindness toward widows, I have found, and I have learned to just accept it. I stop talking. I take pieces of the orange that Molly has found for me, and I smile at her.

"Let's find the group," I say. "I don't want you to miss the end of the tour."

"Mom," she says.

The man is the trainer in the fitness center. His name is Tom.

He and Molly walk me down the hall to the health center, where a nurse takes my blood pressure. She reports it is very low.

Molly ends up finishing the tour with another admissions guide. She tells them that our car is parked at a meter and our time is running out.

Security personnel move the car to an Emmanuel lot. It has not escaped any of these people that their admissions staff left an unconscious woman on the basement floor in an empty hallway with her teenage daughter to fend for herself. They are making nice, and I appreciate that.

While Molly is out of the room the nurse calls in a dean, and the two of them, and Tom, and the security man who moved my car and a man I can't identify all try to persuade me to check myself into the emergency room at the hospital next door, Beth Israel Deaconess. I don't want to spend the time or the money, and I am unconvinced that there is anything physically wrong with me.

They persist. They offer a ride to the hospital and a pick-up when I am discharged. They ensure my car will be safe.

"I'll think," I say, stalling, waiting for my blood pressure to rise.

I am sure they are worried that I am a liability; that I could walk out the door and collapse on their pavement. I am so desperate to leave that I tell them about taking the Trazadone and the Ativan.

"It's just the pills," I say.

This only makes things worse. Molly comes back and agrees to drive to Judy's house, where we are staying the night. Then the nurse takes Molly into the hallway, where they whisper. When they come back, the nurse says, "Go to the hospital. Get checked out. Do it for Molly."

This works. We get in the damn security van, and the campus officer drives us through a mix of streets. We learn he is a retired Boston police officer. This makes me feel guilty for all the times I have called campus security "campus Cub Scouts."

In the ER I am whisked into the triage area so fast you'd think I was dying. There are blood tests, urine tests, and then a string of clinicians comes by with the same questions, over and over. "So, what brings you here?" "So, you fainted?" "Has this ever happened to you before?" and on and on. I bare my soul to each of them, telling them about Ed, the Ativan. Somehow, we are able to make light of it, Molly and I. We smile at one another, like this is our little secret.

About two hours later, I am finally released, having promised to see my own doctor on Monday. The Emmanuel security guard drops us off at our car. Molly takes the wheel, and drives through the brightly lit city, over the new suspension bridge, in three lanes of highway traffic until we get to Judy's one-way street, where she asks me to parallel park. This, I can do.

The next day, I am sitting at Ed's mother's dining room table, relating the events of our Emmanuel tour to Peg. I wish now I was back in the hospital, in the psych ward, sedated. I wish a retired Boston cop was going to pick me up and take me home. I wish Ed was here.

I am crying and so very tired. I lay my head on Peg's table, and I tell her I've made a doctor's appointment for Monday.

"I know, Janice," she says. "I know how you feel. I got sick when my Ed died. I got sick just like you."

I can't stop crying. My forehead rests on the table in the place where my plate would be if this was regular life and I was here for dinner.

"I don't think I should let you drive home," Peg says.

I do drive home. And on Monday, I drive to the doctor. When she tells me I am anemic, and I should take iron. I am disappointed. I thought maybe, just maybe, I had cancer, too.

Chapter Thirteen

Molly has gone out to dinner with her father, and I heat up a pot of chicken soup. I get a nice bowl from the china cabinet and a cloth napkin. But where to sit? Alone at the dining table that seats six or on the sofa? I choose the latter, flanked by Ed's urn and his favorite chair. I take a spoonful of soup and soon I have escalated to full meltdown.

I call Bonni. "What are you doing?" I ask.

She is making dinner. I choke out, "You are doing normal things? You are making dinner for your family?"

She tells me I will be okay. She invites me over, but I decline. I tell her I just want to cry for a minute, and then I ask her, "Bonni, is this really happening? Is Ed really gone?"

I need her to shift the world back onto a level plane.

Her voice is gentle and kind, but she assures me that, yes, Ed is gone.

I can hear her rattling dishes and pots and pans, and I know she is too polite to say she has to go.

"I'll let you go now, Bons. I just needed a reality check. Sometimes I just can't tell what's real."

I sob for a time after we've hung up, and then I text Molly and ask her to let me know when she is on her way home. She texts back that she is almost home, so I rush to the bathroom, wash my face and brush my hair.

When she arrives, flushed from the cold, I am Normal Mom. We watch TV. I don't know who I think I'm fooling.

I am still somewhat weak from the iron deficiency, but at 2 p.m., I have got to get out of the house. I've been on the edge of meltdown all day, and I think going for a run will help.

I start my regular route around the neighborhood, through quiet residential streets. I run comfortably for almost a mile.

At the end of the first loop, which takes me past the front of our house again, I see that there are lights on inside, and I wonder if Ed might be home. I think I should stop to check. I look in our front windows. I start to cry. A cramp has taken hold, so I walk a bit; I've learned it is impossible to run and cry at the same time. I start to rant.

Ed, where are you? I want you to be home. I can't fucking stand this.

I manage to shake off these thoughts and run steadily for at least a mile and a half. Then I pass Ed's dentist's office, and I am tormented by the urge to stop in and ask, "Is Ed Godleski here? I can't find him anywhere." And then I am sobbing again and suddenly, Ed is with me.

Janice, it's okay. It's going to be okay. It is his deep, warm voice. There is no mistaking.

Where are you? I say out loud.

I'm right here. I'm with you. I'm holding you. I'm keeping you safe. I am loving you. More every day.

I know it is Ed because he adds that I should have gotten a receipt for his gun. I laugh and tell him I will.

I run again, and my mind wanders to a conversation I once had with God. I told God he could challenge me, that I could handle a crisis.

I take it back.

Please, give Ed back to me. And don't take anything else away.

I am home now, about to turn the door handle. Suddenly, I am sure Ed will be inside when I walk in, reading his email or tinkering with something, and he will look up and ask if we can have a tea together and talk about our day.

I open the door. He is not in his chair. I collapse in it and cry some more.

It is time to go get Eli at day care. When I have my arms around his little body, I start to weep again, but this time it is from the relief that seeing him brings me. I kiss his face again and again.

"Hi, Nini," he says, smiling. He smells like food.

Eli's care provider, Louise, gives me his shoes and his mini hoodie. I know she sees my tears. I hate when people don't know about Ed, and I hate to tell them. I debate the matter and then blurt, "My husband died recently. I don't know if Sally told you."

"I'm sorry," she says. "Sally mentioned that. I'm so sorry."

Louise puts her hand on my shoulder, and tears drip down my cheeks.

"It's been a hard day," I say, voice trembling. I want to sit down on her couch with Eli. I want Louise to be my day care provider. We could drink tea and do puzzles with the children. She could prepare my lunch and put me down for a nap when I start to cry.

Instead, I take him to the elementary school a block away, thinking we will play on the playground. It's a lovely afternoon.

When we pull in the parking lot, he says, "Backetball." He is pointing to three basketball courts. A father with a slew of boys is playing on one of them, and Eli is walking toward the boys, repeating "basketball, basketball, basketball."

When we get close, I stop him and tell him he can watch but can't play. He stands there, feet spread apart. Five minutes pass. Seven. He is still watching. His head follows the ball.

A new player arrives, and as he retrieves his ball from his trunk, I notice he has an extra in there, and I ask if Eli can play with it.

"This one's flat," he tells me, and I laugh and say, "He won't know the difference."

The young man heads for an empty court, playing a little one-on-nobody. He is quick, and he sinks the ball two out of three times. Eli is transfixed.

"Pass the ball to Nini," I tell him, and he does. I shoot, score, and the half-flat ball lands with a thud. Eli tries to dribble, and the ball works well enough for him. We repeat our game over and over. It reminds me of my brothers playing basketball as kids in the backyard. It feels good to have something feel familiar.

The basketball player has taken a shine to Eli.

"Hey little guy," he says. "What's your name?" Eli plays shy, so I say, "Eli."

I ask the young man's name. Abdul.

Abdul hands Eli the ball, and Eli shyly "passes" it back.

Abdul dances off for more of his rapid-fire play. Eli watches. The sun sets.

"Want to go home and see Daddy?" I ask.

"Go home see Dada," Eli confirms.

We thank Abdul and he and Eli high five.

We say goodbye as we walk to the car. I feel good. Whole. As we drive away, I think how much I love Eli. I love Sally. I love Abdul. I love Abdul's mother. I love this afternoon.

I recognize it as God-given.

Chapter Fourteen

I may not drink alcohol, but I have developed a serious addiction to Nyquil and Ativan.

Every night at bedtime, I take 4 milligrams of Ativan and 2 tablespoons of Nyquil. Eight months ago, this cocktail would have knocked me out. Now it takes at least an hour for the combination to make my head loll.

My psychologist, Barry, suggested this potion after the Trazadone incident that landed me at Beth Israel Deaconess. "If Nyquil works," he said, "use it."

So I do.

Judy has a party one night at her sister's house in East Longmeadow. It's a card party, meaning she is selling the beautiful cards she makes, ones with brilliant photographs on the fronts. I am so grateful to Judy, and I love her cards, so I buy 110 of them.

I look around the room and spot Judy's niece, Shannon, who's in her 30s.

"Want to sneak in the den and talk?" I ask.

"I'd love to," she says. "I don't know anyone here."

I know her mother passed away 18 months ago, so I ask how she is managing, and just like that, we are talking about our grief. I tell her I have heard from Ed; she says she has just started dreaming about her mother. She loves the dreams. She and her mother talk together in them.

We talk for hours. When I leave, I tell Shannon I'm going home to drug myself to sleep. She laughs. She thinks I'm kidding.

When the girls and I moved into our new house on North Maple Street, I promised each of them a pet. Sally got two kittens and named them Ricky and Lucy. One afternoon, Lucy was hit by a car in front of our house. She died in the waiting room of the vet's office, and Sally, who had suffered more than enough loss in her young life with the divorce and accidental deaths of several friends, was beside herself. She decided Ricky could no longer go outside.

Ricky, though, was having none of this new rule. I eventually had to explain to Sally that Ricky would prefer to have a life outdoors with risk than to live a long life on the wrong side of the smells, animals and action. After several weeks, she agreed.

I remember this story because I am thinking about how I would feel if Ed were to come back to me. I wouldn't want to let him out either.

Of course I know that this means I have not graduated into psychiatrist Elisabeth Kübler-Ross' stage of acceptance. I am still in denial. Every day a litany of questions runs through my head: Was I married to Sally and Molly's father? Did a carpenter come? Did I fall in love with him? Did I save his life twice? Then did he die anyway? I know the answers are yes, save the last one. That answer is maybe. I'm still bargaining. I am skirting anger because I'm not sure who to be angry at; dying was not Ed's plan, and God can't blanket all our loved ones in safety. I begin to marvel at how Kübler-Ross pinpointed well the names of the stages of grief in her book "On Death and Dying": denial, anger, bargaining, depression and acceptance. I know that people do not travel through these stages neatly, one by one, until they graduate into acceptance. There is a roller coaster, and I am on it, screaming, going through denial, bargaining and depression over and over and sometimes all at once.

I decide I want to learn more from Kübler-Ross, and I order three more books from Amazon.com. When they arrive, I set "On Death and Dying" aside. I have been through this, so it can wait. I am left to choose between "On Grief and Grieving" and "On Life After Death." The latter might explain how it is that Ed drops in on me on occasion, so I read the whole thing during one long, scalding hot bath. I am transfixed.

Kübler-Ross has a phrase for the conversations I have been having with Ed, "thought transference." Since I have made God so absent in my life of late, I feel blessed to have Kübler-Ross. Her book has become my Bible. I should pray to her.

I still have questions, though.

What of reincarnation? There is much talk of butterflies, a symbol of reincarnation. But I don't want an Ed butterfly. I cannot hold a butterfly.

Can Ed come back to me in another man's body? When? How soon? How will I know?

What if, some day, I actually find I can fall in love, and I remarry? How will we all be together in heaven?

There are only a few people I can discuss these questions with, but no one has answers. One good friend simply tells me, "Trust in God." But that doesn't work for me. I see God's good works in my friends, in the kind acts of strangers, in the beautiful fall weather. But since Ed died, I have not felt him in my own life.

I Google "reincarnation." I learn that in ancient times, reincarnation was considered a curse; ultimate nirvana was achieved only when one escaped from the wheel of rebirth. I learn other things I don't want to hear as well. Tibetan Buddhists, for example, think that people return only as animals. Some believe that the soul cannot reincarnate for at least 1,000 years.

I begin to study men, to see if they have Ed in their eyes. I need to believe he is coming to rescue me. I am stuck in denial. In bargaining.

It's mid-winter, and Molly and I are in New Hampshire for a lacrosse showcase. Young female athletes are everywhere, and I am watching Molly on an indoor field. It is busy, noisy, full of action in here.

"Which one is Molly?" It is Ed. I forget everything else.

"You're here," I say. I am smiling.

"Of course I am. Which one is she?"

"Number 111. In the white pinnie."

He says, "Tell Molly she's doing a good job. She looks great out there."

And then he is gone. I accept it now, that Ed comes and goes in this way, but I hate it.

Ed does not return to me at the Hampshire Dome, but on the second day, there is a man standing next to me wearing blue jeans, a gray sweatshirt and a green Carhart vest. I forget for a moment that Ed is dead, and I think this is him, next to me. Just as quickly, I remember. I get teary. I focus on the game, on Molly. But every now and then, I look at the man's thin leather shoes. "Ed would never wear those shoes," I think.

I make the mistake of telling Molly, in earshot of her friends, that "Ed said to tell you you looked great."

"Mom, stop it," she says.

In the car, I return to the subject. I remind Molly of my near-death experience when I was her age. I tell her how I believe in life after death. I believe that Ed can speak to me, that I can channel him, just not at my whim. She nods. I tell her about the guy in the green Carhart vest, and she says, "I saw him too. I thought he was Ed." I feel better for a moment.

On the highway, driving home, I have a vision of Ed in the hospital bed on his last day, mucus puddling in his cheek, his breathing strained, eyes closed.

"No," my mind shouts. "That DID NOT happen." Panic sets in. We are an hour from home. It is dark. I ask Molly to change the music. She puts on my CDs.

Every goddamn song makes me weepy. How did I not notice that the major themes of my favorite music are love and loss? I keep reaching for the forward button, skipping songs. I am severely agitated and glad Molly can't see me in the darkness. But I need her. I want her to wake up and tell me stories. To talk about school, lacrosse, anything. I need distraction.

I pass through a narrow construction zone.

"Jesus Christ," I yell out loud.

In Greenfield, I spot the exit sign for the Bridge of Flowers. I remember when

I took Ed there, and he couldn't walk back to the car. I have to force my eyes away from the sign, but I can't force my mind away from the thought. Almost there, I keep thinking. Get Molly home.

At our exit, 10 or 15 minutes from home, I pull over and ask Molly to drive the rest of the way.

At home, Molly jumps in the shower. I run outside and let myself go, sobbing, gasping for breath, shouting for Ed, pleading, drooling. The vision of him dying in his bed plays over and over in my head. I call Judy.

"Did that really happen?" I ask her.

There is a pause, then, "Yes, Buggy. It did."

"You were there. You saw it?" I keen.

"Yes, and it sucks, Bug. It's awful. Hideous. It's surreal for me too, but I'm so sorry. It's real."

Judy is quiet. I know she doesn't know what to say. I also know I need to let her go. She was eating dinner with her sister and brother when I called. I have become a burden.

I am on the back deck, on a long bench Ed built, phone to my ear, head hung between my knees. I feel movement to my right and look up to see Sally and Eli. I tell Judy that they are here, and hang up.

"What's wrong?" Sally asks me, noticing my state of mind.

"I'm okay," I say. "I do this every day."

She puts Eli on my lap, and I hold both of them and cry and cry. In the dark, Eli can't see my face, and he laughs as I shudder and gasp. He thinks we are playing a game.

For the rest of the night, I make short trips outside to continue my collapse. I hide in the bathroom. I take a long shower. I keep hearing Molly's therapist tell me, "It's okay to fall apart," but it feels awful.

I cover Molly with my grandmother's down quilt that night and kiss her forehead. Even so, I can't help feeling that she is the mother, and I am the child.

The next night, I am determined to cook dinner, chicken wraps, a favorite of Molly's. I ask her to stop at the store on her way home from work to get the tortillas.

When she arrives home, she also has a bottle of juice. "Nourishment for the brain," it says on the label. She pours herself a glass. Maybe she is thinking it will help her with SATs, but I also consider the possibility that she didn't buy it for herself.

I have therapy with Melissa every Tuesday at 2 p.m. I wish she was on call for each new, unsettling emotion. I want to live in her office above Sylvester's restaurant in downtown Northampton. But I have 50 minutes every seven days.

I drive there, fast, climb the three flights of stairs. Greetings are minimal because I must launch into my woes. I cry. I blow my nose. I fill her wicker trash basket with gooey tissue. I trust her with my awfulness.

I tell every detail of every story from the week, in chronological order. She listens. She is so happy when I tell her I have heard from Ed or felt his presence. I love that she loved Ed, too.

I can feel when the clock is nearing 2:50. I always squeeze in one last thought. Then I stand, hand her a check for $25, and walk down the stairs. I always feel just a bit lighter.

I am talking to Judy on the phone, and she tells me how much she hates her job.

"Quit," I say. "I told you I will support you." It is not a practical offer. I have very little money in the bank and with each mortgage payment I worry about how much longer I can stay in the house. I make the offer anyway.

I love Judy so much I want to help her. I hate to see her working 10- and 12-hour days. I am sure she will laugh and change the subject, but instead she says, "Well, what you said before is that I could come work for Beetle Press."

"I did?" I say. I can't remember this, but I love the idea. "Let's do it."

She says she will give her notice tomorrow and her last day will be just before Thanksgiving. We decide that Judy will try to find clients that need our writing and graphic design services in the Boston area. We are full of good ideas.

Chapter Fifteen

I believe in Ed.

I believe in one Ed,

His sons' Father, my Almighty,

Disbeliever in heaven, lover of earth,

And all that is, seen and unseen.

I believe in one Beautiful Ed Godleski,

The only Son of Ed senior

Eternally begotten of his Father,

God from God, Light from Light,

True God from true God,

Never forgotten, but made,

Of one Being with the Father.

Through him all things were safe.

For me and my salvation

He visits from heaven:

By the power of His Parents

He was born at Cooley Dickinson Hospital,

And became a man.

For no one's sake, he was riddled with lung cancer;

He suffered death and was cremated.

On the third day, I seriously waited for him to rise again

In accordance with the Scriptures;

(After all, he had "God" in his name, and he *was* a carpenter)

Instead, he ascended into heaven

And is seated at the right hand of his father.

I hope he will come again in glory; he would never judge the living or the dead, and his life ever after will have no end.

I believe in the Holy Spirit, the Lord, the giver of life,

And I believe in Ed.

With the Father and Son, Ed is worshiped and glorified.

He speaks to me through Emmett and Eli and through the picture on the wall.

I believe in one holy catholic and apostolic Church.

I acknowledge one baptism for the forgiveness of sins.

I look for the resurrection of my husband,

So I will have life in the world to come. Amen.

I have bastardized the Nicene Creed. It's not that I have given up on God. I just don't feel him. When I reach for comfort, I look to Ed.

I try to make room for God, but Ed seems to be taking all the space in my heart. When I finally make it back to church one Sunday, I do feel some connection to God during the prayers of the people. But when they pray for those who have gone before us, I think of Ed, and the heavy curtain of grief falls. God has been edged out.

I know God is with me, that I could not be on this journey without him. I see him in Roger, the electrician, who has now come three times to make small repairs. I see him in my friends, who call me daily, who cook for me, who wake up at sunrise to walk with me, who pull me out of weepy funks and take me to the movies. I see God in my daughters' strength, and I see God in Tommy, who continues to help me around the house.

When I hike with my friend Deirdre, another widow I have been stalking, we talk about our lost husbands. Deirdre tells me she has a totally different relationship with her husband than she did 12 years ago, when he died. She says they talk all the time. I tell her about my conversations with Ed, about how I feel him with me often.

We talk about God, and we see God everywhere as we hit the summit of the Notch and look out over Amherst, Belchertown, South Hadley and Northampton far in the distance.

Being with Deirdre, who I met seven years ago in church, gives me time to reflect on God and also time to understand that I am not crazy. I am a lost, grieving wife.

We swap stories about how we might find our husbands. Deirdre has had 12 long years to work this out. She is convinced her beloved Gary is working for the CIA and can't contact her. When he has completed his mission, he will come back home.

We laugh when she tells me this. We know we are both kidding, but we are serious, too. There are parts of us that still need to believe these stories, to still have hope. I have faith that one day I will find God again. And I have faith that one day, too, I will find Ed.

A thought: Since I am rewriting Scripture, I consider this:

Ed has died.

Ed is not risen.

Will Ed come again?

Time. Watching time pass. That's what some days are about. I wake up, and the clock says 6:25. I slam my hand on the snooze. I wrestle myself out of bed. Molly has been up for 45 minutes. We both know she doesn't need me to help her get ready, but we both also know, in a way that goes unspoken, that she needs to see that I will not stay in my bed all day, weeping and drooling and blowing my nose.

I make coffee and retrieve the paper from the front walkway. I offer to make her breakfast. "No thanks." Lunch? "No." And I sign checks — for the cafeteria, for the lacrosse program, for the therapist, the tutor, the SAT administrator.

After Molly has left in a whir and a rush, I look for jobs in the paper's Help Wanted section. There are none. There never are.

The clock reads 7:46. Now what?

Email helps. I hear from former colleagues, fast friends, and I am starting to get requests to write for the *Daily Hampshire Gazette*. This is good. I need something to do, and I need money.

I am in an endless loop of frustration with Ed's life insurance company, which appears to be searching for a way to get out of paying. Each day I call the claims investigator to let him know I am not going away. I call a woman named Heather at our former pharmacy's corporate office because this pharmacy is one of the reasons the life insurance company hasn't completed its investigation. It wants Ed's prescription records from several years ago. It has heard the same facts from his primary care physician, his oncologist and his radiation oncologist: Ed had cancer, was diagnosed in May and died in September. What more does the insurance company need to know?

Heather has stopped returning my calls. I call her every day, anyway.

It is twilight, and I am frightened about how I will I pay my bills, how I will keep my house. Will I ever find a job? I have talked Judy into quitting the job she hated to work with me to grow Beetle Press, promising to pay her for six months. Will I have to blow through my entire savings to stay afloat?

Again, I am awash in tears, saliva.

I go upstairs to the bathroom, and in the mirror I see what grief is doing to my face. I have aged 10 years. I don't care.

I take my four milligrams of Ativan and struggle to open a new bottle of Nyquil. It has a push-and-turn top, and the push tabs won't be pushed.

I keep pushing and turning. Nothing. I grow frantic. "Christ," I yell. "Fuck."

Then it opens. I take my shot, feel the heat as it slithers down my throat, and I head for bed. I try not to think about how I will wean myself off all this shit.

"I just want to be normal," I cry to Ed on the wall. "When will I be normal?"

At the end of my weekly session with Melissa, as I am writing out the check, I tell her that Ed's death really was beautiful.

"I know," she says. "I felt that when I was there."

"When you were where?" I say.

"At your house."

I don't know what she is talking about. Melissa has never been to my house.

Melissa tells me that she came to the house to see me the day before Ed died. I stare blankly at her. My time is up, and I have to go. So, later, I call her on the phone. She tells me that Ed and I had an appointment on Monday, the last day that Ed was alive, and I had called the Friday before to tell her we wouldn't be able to make it.

"I asked if you wanted me to come by the house, and you asked me to call you," Melissa said. "When I called you, you asked if I would come over for a session at home on Monday instead."

I don't remember any of it.

In the next session, I ask Melissa to tell me more. Ed was on the hospital bed, unconscious, with Lee close by, she says. I was on the couch.

"I got the sense he was kind of awake, shifting," she tells me. "I said Hi, told him he was great and that I cared about him and about you. You asked Lee to stay sitting with him and suggested we go out on the gazebo. You gave me a little tour of the yard on the way out there."

I can see that now. I can see us walking down the steps to the deck and crossing to the brick walkway. I can see myself telling Melissa about the carnations I planted for Ed because his grandmother used to grow them.

"You were very worried about being alone. You cried. You said you needed to write a book to grieve. When I left, I promised Ed I would continue to see you and stay connected. He was starting to get really restless."

"Was Kisha on the gazebo when we got out there?"

"Yes," she says. "She wasn't happy about having to leave it either."

And I remember, but it's as if I am recalling scenes from a movie, rather than my life.

"How come I didn't remember, Melissa?"

She shrugs. She does not say, "Because you are drugging yourself."

As I think back on that last week with Ed, I realize I don't remember much at all. I need to remember.

Chapter Sixteen

The lacrosse coach at Plymouth State University has invited Molly to visit the campus in the fall of 2010. We drive to New Hampshire to take her up on that offer.

I wake Molly up as we near the exit. We see the athletics building and the new hockey rink from the off-ramp. Then we cross the Pemigewasset River and find ourselves at a quaint rotary with the loveliest downtown. The campus is set at the top of a hill just beyond.

"Look, there's a bakery," I say. "And a hardware store, and a used book store and an antique store. Ed would love it here. I think this could be it, Molly."

We drive around the rotary and through town a few more times. "Do you feel it?" I ask.

She says she does, and I don't think she is humoring me.

When we park in the lot, it seems there are green Jeeps like Ed's in every spot.

"Molly," I say. "Look at all the Jeeps."

"Mom. Stop."

We meet the lacrosse coach, Kristen, and she and Molly talk in her office. Molly spends the night on campus with lacrosse players and drinks beer at a baseball team party. I stay at my parents' house, about 40 minutes away, and in the morning we meet up with Molly and Kristen and the players and other recruits. We walk across campus, my mother admiring the brick buildings and the truly charming New England campus. I am so pleased they want my girl.

When my parents leave, Molly and I have lunch at a diner that looks like a dining car, just like Miss Flo's in Florence. The whole town has a we're-in-Florence-and-feel-right-at-home quality. I can't help telling Molly again that Ed would love it.

While we wait for our food, I gaze out the window at the campus. I want Ed to be part of this.

And then I have an epiphany.

I realize I never said goodbye to him. I never told him how much I would miss him.

I've figured out why I am so anguished.

As I drive home, Molly falls asleep, her feet on the dashboard. I'm content behind the wheel, listening to the CDs I have played relentlessly since Ed died — Kasey Chambers, Norah Jones, the Guess Who. The songs are like lullabies.

As I drive I think about how I can say goodbye to Ed. I had so many chances to tell him, to touch his face and say, "I love you, honey. Goodbye." Why didn't I?

I remember the night I read him Sally and Molly's letters and asked, "Did you hear me?" and he did not answer. I asked, over and over, "Did you hear me? Did you hear me? Did you hear me?" until he said, with his last reserve of energy, "I heard you." I had a full day and a night and two hours and 40 minutes of time with Ed after that but I didn't speak another word to him until he was taking his last breaths.

I think about saying goodbye to Ed along the river's edge, where we released his ashes. But it is too cold, and the boat is no longer in the water. I think about sitting on the floor in the living room with his urn, but that seems staged. I think I might drive to Ed's old house in Hatfield, or to the Poet's Seat Tower in Greenfield. But nothing seems right.

And then, staring out my window at the sun struggling to break through the clouds, I realize I don't have to say goodbye to Ed. He is still with me and always will be. Goodbye is not necessary.

And then — my third epiphany on this day — I realize that everything's going to be okay. I am going to survive this. Molly will survive. We will all be okay, just as I told Ed in those final moments when he took those last breaths, so shallow and slow. "It's okay," I told him. "Everything's going to be okay."

It is huge, this revelation in my car. It is all going to be okay.

I remain traumatized, and I continue to worry about whether Beetle Press can support Judy and me, whether I can keep my house. There are many tears, but it is all different somehow.

When I cry, I am not hysterical. I am simply intensely sad. I have more aware-ness. I notice the tears as they fall from my eyes. Each one looks the same — a huge drop, distinct, oval. I watch them drip onto my desk or the marble coffee table Ed made. If I don't wipe them up, they leave salty, circular patches.

I am sitting in my living room in early November 2010. It has only been two months since Ed died, and I am fretting over money but also over Ed's last week of life. I can't remember anything I said or did. I am trying to produce a memory when the phone rings. It is Pat Riggs, the director of the Hospice program. I attended the first week of a Hospice bereavement group she put together and never went back. Pat wants to know why, and asks if I am okay.

"No," I say. "I am not okay."

"Do you want to come back to the group?" she asks me.

"No, thank you," I say. "But I would love to talk to Ed's nurses. I can't remember those last days, and I want to remember."

"Can I have Julia and Eileen call you?" she asks me.

"Please," I say. "And the Reiki woman. The volunteer. Can I talk to her, too?"

For my birthday in November, Molly gives me a journal about Ed's last week. This is what I asked her for. When Ed's breathing became harsh and difficult, she writes, "It scared me and you." Sally gives me a bracelet that has a slot for a photo, and I put a picture of Ed at his party in August inside it. Sally makes my birthday dinner. It makes me feel like a good mother, because I have raised these thoughtful girls.

Bonni gives me a gorgeous velour scarf with a note that I should think of it as Ed wrapping his arms around me. She also gives me a photo of Ed, taken at our wedding, which she has placed in a wooden star. Around it, she has created a beautiful mosaic with tile and beads.

"It's for your Christmas tree," she says.

I love the star, but I don't put it on our Christmas tree. I put it on the piano, next to the urn. Now I have an Ed in every room, as well as the bracelet with the photo of him, which I wear constantly. Judy is the only one I tell that there is also an Ed on the bathroom door. I see his face in one particular knot of wood. She does not.

The day before Thanksgiving is the first time I have gone grocery shopping in years. Ed did all the shopping. I have a dozen people coming for dinner, and I'm terrified that I will forget something, that I won't have everything I'll need. It takes me an hour to get through the store and when I get home and start to cook, I am so overwhelmed that I call Mary.

"Do you want me to come over?" she asks.

I say that I do.

In the evening, Ed's oldest son Jack arrives to make Gramma's traditional bean casserole in the kitchen. With Mary's help, I have made two apple pies, a casserole of vegetables, vegetarian stuffing, for Kisha, and meat stuffing.

Jack tells me that Gramma didn't want me to host Thanksgiving because she was worried about my health. I tell Jack I am fine.

"But Gramma said you are sick. She said you came to her house. That you fell asleep on her dining room table."

"I did not," I say. I can't imagine why Peg has told Jack this.

He repeats what he said. I repeat my denial.

Then I have a flash. I am sitting in her dining room, crying, dumping my woes on her, and then laying my head on her table, my eyes so heavy, closing. I remember her alarm, and that she said, "I don't know if I should let you drive home."

Just like that, I remember.

Thanksgiving day is beautiful, full of family – my children, Tommy and his brother and sister and Peg, Jack, Lee, Ana, Ry, Kisha and Emmett. Ry and Kisha have to drive back home to Beverly, and they look shell-shocked. I learned several days ago that Kisha is expecting another baby. It makes me sad that Ed will have a grandchild he has never met.

Lee looks so much like Ed that I can't take my eyes off him. When he puts his arm around Ana on the couch, I am actually jealous. Where is my Ed? Where is his arm around me?

Ry has on Ed's shoes, the ones he wore at our wedding. I gave them to Ry the day after Ed died.

"I like your shoes, Ry," I tell him.

He says "Thanks." A moment later, when the meaning behind the compliment has registered, he says it again: "Thanks."

It is nice to have all the children together. And as they all leave, it is like losing them again after Ed died. It is like losing Ed again.

I go to bed; my girls and Tommy stay up a little later.

Honey. The kids were here, and they are great. But Ry is stressed, honey. He is working too hard, and they are having another baby, and where are you?

Ed tells me, "I'm with Ry. He needs me now."

After Thanksgiving, I am sick. I take an Ativan and fall back to sleep. When I wake, I am shaky, weak, sick to my stomach.

I had plans with a friend, and call her to say I'm not well enough to see her.

"Lauren, I don't feel up to it," I say. I start to cry.

"Do you want to get together tomorrow?" she asks.

"I have plans with someone. I can't remember who," I say, knowing I sound evasive. Then I ask, "What day is today?"

"Saturday," she says.

"I thought it was Friday?"

"Nope."

My crying escalates. "Then the plans I had were with you."

I go back to bed. By Monday, it occurs to me that I am not sick. I am detoxing from the Ativan because I haven't taken it during the day since the day before our turkey feast. I call my doctor, who tells me the only thing to do is take more Ativan. I call the psychiatrist who prescribed it, and he also tells me to simply take more.

I refuse. It's time to stop this. But the psychiatrist says I must taper off, and he's outlined a plan that will take a month to enact. By mid-December, three months after Ed's death, I will be drug free.

"When will I feel better?" I ask.

"Not soon," he says.

"A month?"

"Probably more."

The next day, in bed, I cannot believe the intensity of my discomfort. If I didn't know I wasn't dying — having a stroke or a heart attack — I would be dialing 911. Instead, I use the laptop and Google "Ativan withdrawal."

I learn that Ativan is stored in the body's fat cells and that withdrawal symptoms include a racing heart, trembling and anxiety. In some cases withdrawal can cause death.

Jack's girlfriend, Louise, rides over on her bike one afternoon. As we talk over tea, I tell her that I have been recreating Ed's last days, because I can't remember.

"You can't remember what?" she asks.

"Where I was. What I was doing. I can't remember if I took good care of him."

Louise tells me this: "You weren't there. Only a part of you was there. You were working on muscle memory. You were doing things you knew you needed to do. You were in Ed's bed all the time. If you weren't there, you were in the room or in one of the adjacent rooms."

Several days later, I have just gotten out of the bath and am wearing the clothes

Ed died in — his red lounging pants and a soft thermal jersey — when one of the Hospice nurses, Julia, returns my call.

"What are you looking for?" she asks.

"I don't know," I say. "I need to know that I took good care of him."

This is what she says:

"You were there Janice. You were amazingly attentive. You kept him free of pain, and you managed all of the details that needed to take place, and you were loving him. And he knew it."

All I can remember about Kathi, the Reiki volunteer, is the gratitude I felt when she visited Ed on the last day he was alive. I remember the labored sound of his breathing. I remember there were many people in the house, but I can't see their faces. I remember looking through the Yellow Pages for a funeral home. I hope Kathi can tell me more.

When she arrives, I recognize her immediately. She is my height, perhaps a bit older, and her hair is thick, blond and shoulder-length. I hug her and make tea.

"What is it you're looking for?" Kathi asks.

"I want to remember that day," I say.

"There was so much love in this room," Kathi says. "It was so sad, but it was so beautiful, too."

She says that when she arrived she asked me if I was Ed's daughter, and I snapped at her, and God, I remember. I remember being angry with her because Ed was not old. He was frail and sick.

"I'm sorry that I was cross with you."

"Oh no, no no. You were fine," she says.

Then she tells me that she asked us — Ed's boys, my girls — if Ed had favorite music, and we said he loved music. And she noticed the piano and asked if anyone played, and Lee said he did, and I realize that that is why Lee was playing the piano.

Kathi says Lee played for three hours and then Ed grew calm, and I asked her where I was, and she tells me, "In his bed."

"For how long?"

"For those three hours," she says. "You were so adoring."

I begin telling friends that I'm having trouble remembering, and I ask them to send me stories about Ed.

"I brought flowers in a vase," my friend Maria says. "I had been thinking of you and wanting to do something, so I brought flowers from our garden."

Suddenly, I see them. They were brilliant pinks and yellows in a glass vase that I put on the piano.

"Where was I when you got here?" I ask.

She points to the piano stool. "You must have been sitting down there," she says. "I could only see your face."

Hours later, I am puzzling over Maria's story. I remember Maria coming in the front door, calling to us. Where was I? Was I on the piano stool? That doesn't make sense.

But then it comes to me. I see where I was. I was on the couch, underneath Ed, his thin body on top of mine, his head on my chest.

Only my face was showing.

Chapter Seventeen

The very second I am on the verge of awareness each morning, I remember, I know, that Ed is gone. On this morning, I slide my index finger through Ed's ring. I have worn it on a chain around my neck since he died. I am holding on. I have been so aware that my spiritual life died with Ed, and I don't want to lose faith.

One day, when I am out running, I start to recite the Lord's Prayer. I think I can do this much. What happens is I pick it apart.

Our Father. I study this phrase. He is my father.

Who art in heaven. I stare up at the sky. Wonder, "Ed, are you up there?"

Hallowed be thy name. God. Yes. The name itself is so blessed.

Thy Kingdom come. What does this mean? Where is the Kingdom coming? Or does it mean to the Kingdom we all will go? Yes, I think so.

Thy will be done. This was not born of anyone's will, not even God's. I don't be-lieve that.

On Earth. Right here.

As it is in heaven. It must be so much nicer there. That is where I want to go. I just can't yet. I need to take care of my daughters. I need to take care of Eli. But I can't take care of myself. I have no money. I have no job. I have no sense of who I am. I am stuck, but here I am, moving.

In bed, at night, I talk to my Ed on the nightstand, the Maglite trained on his face, his eyes.

I am so sorry I didn't talk to you in your last days. It was so hard for me to talk to you because you didn't talk back. I couldn't bear it. But here I am, talking to you, and you are not talking back. I carry you around with me, Ed, every day. I will carry you with me forever. I wish I had told you that.

It's early December 2010. Only a few months have passed since Ed died, and it seems that every movie I watch, every book I read sends the message that I can find Ed if I learn the right secret. I am sure each movie is being aired so that I will watch it. I am sure that fate has placed each book in my hand.

In "13 Going On 30," Jennifer Garner only needs fairy dust to make a wish, turn back time and be with the man she loves. "Send *me* some of that fairy dust," I say.

In a book I am reading on Molly and Sally's recommendation, the protagonist, a teenage girl at a stuffy private school in London, has special powers. She can envision a door of light and pass through it to a realm in which she can visit with her dead mother. Each night, when I put this book down, I talk to Ed about the day, and I shine the Maglite and stare into his eyes. When I say goodnight, I picture the door of light, but it has not yet let me pass through. I am still standing on this side of the realm.

On my friend Lisa's birthday, I take her to see the latest Harry Potter movie. In it, a man turns a stone over and over and, with the movement, his late wife comes back to him. When I get home, I search to find a river stone that was in Ed's office. I turn it over and over in my hand. He does not come back to me.

In "Inception" I find a message I think will help. Each night Cobb, played by Leonardo DiCaprio, visits his dead wife as he is dreaming. He has practiced this skill and can control his dreams. He desperately wants her back. But at the movie's end, when faced with the choice of living with her in a dream state or being reunited with his children in real life, Cobb chooses his children. The message is so clear to me. I know that I can't have Ed *and* my children, my little Eli. I feel acceptance.

Ed and I saw "Inception" in a movie theater when it was released, even though he was terribly sick. We were exhausted, and we both fell asleep. When I go to bed, I talk to him about it.

Honey, it's good we fell asleep when we went to see "Inception." We couldn't have handled it. We couldn't have handled the prospect of having to choose between each other or our children. I wouldn't trade one of my children to have you back. You wouldn't either. The world is telling me something. I think, to be grateful.

My dishwasher has broken again. I need to shop for Christmas. My savings is dwindling fast. At this rate I will lose my house in four months. I put the little energy I have left into filing a complaint with the Massachusetts Division of Insurance.

I explain that Ed and I took out the policy in November 2008, shortly after we were married. Prudential agents hired its own clinicians to conduct a physical examination, which included a urinalysis, CBC and a test of liver enzymes. I name the agent we purchased the policy from, who told us that the test results indicated that Ed was in excellent physical condition, so much so that the company gave us what was described as "the premium rate."

I summarize Ed's cancer diagnosis and treatment, along with the contact I have had with the agent and the insurance company's investigator. I keep things simple. I don't express my frustration and puzzlement that the company requested pharmacy records from 2007, even though Ed's physicians — and his death certificate — clearly state that the cause of death was cancer, diagnosed in 2010.

I close with this:

I have now waited almost three months, and I have no resolution on my claim. I am fed up. I have been in weekly contact with the company, and over two weeks ago, I was told that the information that the company needed was in hand and that a determination should be forthcoming. On Friday, December 10, 2010, I informed the investigator over the telephone that if I did not receive a determination by the end of day on Monday, December 13, 2010, that I would be filing a claim with the Massachusetts Insurance Division, hence this complaint.

I mail the complaint to the state, and email copies to the agent and investigator. I feel no satisfaction. It is not fun to be a bitch.

The next day, a fellow from A1 Plumbing comes. He is the third person to tackle my damn dishwasher, which now floods the floor whenever it's running. Twenty minutes pass, and he calls me into the kitchen. He's replaced the seal on the pump that a friend and I accidentally dislodged when we tried to fix the dishwasher ourselves, but I can see water flooding on the floor.

"The pump's leaking," he says. "You need a repairman."

"I thought you were the repairman?" I think my mouth is hanging open.

"Oh no," he says. "We don't touch appliances."

He fixes a leak in the kitchen faucet and then tackles another problem, Molly's radiator. I know Ed is with me because I am not freaking out, not cussing at this poor man. I am thinking I will be dishwasher-less and so be it.

I busy myself wrapping gifts. Ten minutes later, the plumber is still upstairs when my cell phone rings. Area code 904. I answer, and it's a woman from the life insurance company.

"We have gathered all of the pertinent medical records regarding your husband."

In my head, I'm saying, "Tell me something I don't know."

And she does. She says the company has approved the claim and is overnighting a check to me.

She keeps talking. I say "Thank you" multiple times. We hang up.

I am holding my head in both hands, relief trying hard to flood in, but it occurs to me then, truly for the first time, that I can only keep my house because Ed is dead. "Oh my God. Oh my God. Oh my God."

I wrestle with this reality for a time then decide to put my guilt aside for now. I decide it is okay to live, to feel financial security, but it is certainly not fair.

I continue with wrapping presents. The plumber has fixed Molly's radiator, and he is leaving. When I am sure he is at the end of the walk, I holler, "Guess what? I'm going to buy a new dishwasher!"

Chapter Eighteen

Lee and Ana come to visit, and afterward, in the car on the way to the train station, Lee says he is still sad, still missing his father so much. Then they ask how I am, and I say I am struggling.

"I don't remember taking care of him," I say. My voice cracks, and I'm irritated at myself.

"You were great," they say, talking over each other.

When we reach the train station, there is the usual chaos as they reach for their bottles of water and backpacks and hustle out of the car.

Ana pulls a sketch book from her bag. "I did some sketches, you know, when Ed was sick."

She hands me the book. I catch my breath.

One sketch shows the marble coffee table with bottles of pills, a syringe. I remember: These are Ed's medications that I gave him on the hour. The coffee table, yes, it was covered with medications.

The second sketch is of Ed, eyes closed. In the third drawing, Lee is at the piano. My eyes settle on the fourth drawing, and I trace it with my fingers as my mind takes me back.

"I rubbed his feet," I say, looking at Ana's sketch of my hands caressing Ed's feet.

"Yes, you did," Ana says.

"And his hands." I am so grateful for this memory, for this missing piece of my life, in front of me in charcoal.

A1 Plumbing's plumber did more than fix the faucet. He recommended the Mill River chapter of Business Network International as a way to grow my business. I've emailed the president of the chapter and will be attending the next meeting. I order a new Beetle Press business card, one that will stand out. It's oversized and offers a list of services.

It is progress.

When I wake up I realize I have dreamt about Ed. He was helping me repair a tire. We were lying on black pavement. Ed was holding the adjustable wrench in his hand, opening it wider and wider to demonstrate how it adjusts, but he opened it so much, the pieces came apart in his hand. Next, I remember, I was lying flat on my back and my shirt was riding up. Ed put an index finger inside my belly button. It tickled. It felt real.

The memory of the dream helps me get moving. I am sleepy but motivated as I sip tea in my Polish pottery mug and drive to Eastworks, the old mill building where BNI meets. I get there at 7 a.m., right on time.

I was expecting a small group in a small room, and am taken aback when I enter a warehouse-sized space teeming with businesspeople. There are people in suits and people in jeans. A man with dreadlocks gives me my name tag.

Everyone is networking, making appointments, swapping business cards, but I can't handle that quite yet. I take a seat and spend 11 minutes studying the agenda and reading the list of member businesses on the back. I forget to drink my tea.

The meeting is brought to order by a man in khakis and a white dress shirt. He is the president I emailed to say I would be visiting the meeting. The men in suits, a lawyer and a tax accountant, will give today's presentation on incorporating a business.

After routine business is taken care of, each member offers a one-minute message for the week. The president tells visitors that after members are done, we will have a chance to speak. There are four of us.

I catch on easily to how it works: you stand to speak, state your name and the name of your business, specify a referral that would be a great fit, and then repeat your name before sitting down. It's like a commercial. I am about to be on the BNI network.

As the talk travels around the room, I suddenly feel shaky. It is almost my turn.

Then the president is gesturing toward me.

I stand.

Here's what I have to keep myself from saying:

"My name is Janice Beetle Godleski. I lost my job at Cooley Dickinson Hospital in September, and four days later, my beloved husband died of cancer. I am totally fucked up, and I'm actually experiencing Ativan withdrawal right now. So don't be concerned if you see me shaking. And, I am a good writer. Think of me. My name is Janice Beetle Godleski."

What I actually say is:

"My name is Janice Beetle Godleski. I'm a writer, editor and production manager. Since 1998, I have operated a business called Beetle Press. A good referral for me would be a marketing supervisor at a college, university, social service agency or start-up business. I look forward to meeting your writing needs. I'm Janice Beetle Godleski."

I sit and feel a sense of hope and accomplishment. The moment was exhilarating, and I want another one. Business carries on, though. I listen closely to the presentation on incorporation. The suits do a great job. It occurs to me that there must be a cost associated with membership. This is too organized. There is too much information, too many resources. It is too much to get for nothing.

I am right about this, and at 8:20, visitors are asked to meet in the hall, where we learn that the annual membership fee is $464 dollars and $25 a month after that. I need to think about it. I head back into the meeting room, ready to network.

I introduce myself to a mortgage lender, since I am about to refinance using the life insurance money, and I talk to a financial advisor. I meet the president, a web designer. I hand out my cards.

I leave ready to grow a business. I am excited about what Judy and I can do together. I feel the promise of resurrection. Everything really is going to be okay.

I dream about an old love, Bobby Dillard. He has heard I lost my husband, and has come to console me. He looks the same, but I can see there is still an edge; he does not forgive me for breaking his heart.

We go on a boat ride and visit a museum. I enjoy Bobby's company, but he is subdued. Still, I am glad he has visited. I collapse when I get out of the car. I am on my knees in a parking lot, and I am whimpering because I can't stand up. My legs don't work. I feel guilty because I know I must ask him for help, but so many years ago, I hurt him.

"Bobby, can you please help me get inside? I can't move."

He lifts me to my feet, his left arm encircling my waist. It feels so good. I melt into him, and then his arm is around my neck, his left hand slips down to cup my breast. I laugh, stunned, and remove it.

Then I realize that this is not Bobby at all. It was Bobby, but he is gone. It is Ed here with me now. I know because of the warmth I feel and because I can't see his face; when I dream about Ed, he is light and air.

I decide to run on the new bike path that runs alongside a local Audubon sanctuary. I run almost two miles before I turn around. On the way back, I look up to see two deer on the path about 50 yards ahead of me. I stop to admire them, and a huge buck comes out of the woods to join them, then a third doe. The buck's antlers are impressive. I know they see me, but they don't run.

"Is one of you Rudolph?" I ask.

I stare. They stare back. Then they wander off into the woods.

"That was a nice Mind Gift, Ed," I say. "Thank you."

Christmas is five days away. Jack calls, and I can tell from his voice he is relieved to have finished his first semester of law school. He is going to Pennsylvania for Christmas to see his mom, so he and I are going to have dinner in Northampton before he leaves.

Lee calls while he's walking to practice with one of the three bands he is in. He tells me that school wrapped up well, and he earned three As and a C+ in math. Math is tough for him, as it was for Ed, even though Ed's dad, Lee's Grampa, was the chair of the Northampton High School math department. Lee says he will get over to celebrate Christmas with us at some point.

On Monday Ry calls to invite me to celebrate Christmas with him, Kisha and Emmett. I am so grateful to be remembered, given my meltdown the last time I was with him. We talk for a long time about his work, where we both are in our grieving and how Kisha is feeling in this new pregnancy. Before we hang up, we decide that I will visit him the week after Christmas.

Ed's mother, Peg, says she wants to stay at her house and do nothing, and I'm trying to respect that. Sally, Tommy, Eli and Darrian, Tommy's older son, are sleeping over on Christmas Eve. I am excited about reading the boys *The Night Before Christmas* and the classic newspaper column, "Yes, Virginia, There Is a Santa Claus."

Yes, Family, there is a Christmas coming to us.

I make my second visit to the BNI group. I know what I'm going to say in my 60 seconds, and I feel confident. I still shake continually, especially in situations that normally produce anxiety, but the doctors' only advice continues to be to take more Ativan, and I am adamantly against that advice. So I suffer the consequences.

I've decided to use my 60 seconds to tell the history of Beetle Press — how it got started and how it's evolved. As the members make their presentations, I hear the squeak of a rubber toy — the sign a speaker has gone over the one-minute limit.

I stand when it is my turn and begin my spiel. I'm not nervous, but as I talk, I begin to tremble. My voice is quivering, too. Then, I hear the rubber toy squeak. I repeat my name and sit, deeply embarrassed.

When the meeting is over, I introduce myself to several more people. I have a marketing idea for Lee, a former electrician who now does massage. Before I can open my mouth, he sees my name tag and asks, "Are you related to the Godleskis in Florence?"

I tell him I was married to Ed Godleski.

"Oh. That means you've had a *hard* year," Lee says. There is compassion and concern in his voice.

He tells me he knew Ed's father from his teaching days. He also knew Jack's mother.

I feel awkward, not entirely in control of my emotions. It is also still weighing on me that I received the squeak for going over my 60 seconds. I am taking that correction much too hard.

At home, I flop on my bed.

Ed, I can't do this. I don't have it in me to work this damn hard. When will I be normal?

I have so many presents to wrap, and no Christmas spirit. It is a labor, not a labor of love. I do Molly's first, then Sally's. I decide Eli's presents are all from Santa so I don't have to wrap them. I wrap Lee's presents, and I get to the one Ed picked out for him last January, when we did our traditional post-holiday shopping. It's an ornament that looks like a tiny accordion, an instrument Lee had been teaching himself to play at the time. I make a note for Lee so he knows his father chose it himself. Then I hit a wall. I look at Ed-On-The-Piano. I know Ed is really gone.

Today is an Eli day, and when I pick him up he is full of energy. Louise, his day care provider, has given him a truck for Christmas, and he can't get enough of playing with it. I have to wrestle him into his coat. It takes many "thank yous" and "goodbyes" and "Merry Christmases" before we make it all the way out the door. Eli says, "No go home see Daddy," so I decide a field trip is in order.

We drive down a long driveway and park behind the hockey rink of a local school. On a recent run, I'd noticed a huge mound of ice and snow back there, presumably dumped there by the Zamboni. "Eli," I tell him. "We're going to play in the snow."

I hand him a piece of ice and say, "Throw it," and he does. He laughs. He throws another chunk, and then another. I do too. He notices that the ice makes his hands cold, but he doesn't care. He loves how the snowy ice explodes when it hits the ground.

For a minute or two, he plays on his own, so I create my own private game. I pick up a huge clump of ice and say, "I want my job back now." On "now," I throw the clump at a stone, and it shatters.

I pick up another piece. "Give me back my husband." I let it fly on "husband." It shatters, too.

Then I take Eli home, and he runs into Tommy's arms. I hug him, loving the smallness of his body within my embrace.

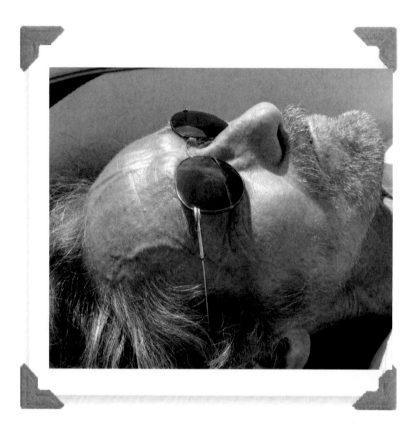

Chapter Nineteen

I've lit candles in the living room as I get ready for friends to come over, and the balsam tree is aglow with the little white lights that are strung on it. Ed smiles down at me from the piano, and I begin to dance. I flutter my scarf in his direction. I blow kisses. I feel like a teenager in love. I almost feel his presence in the room, like he is encouraging me, laughing in his shy way, embarrassed a bit, but loving every minute of my attention.

I suddenly have a profound sense of what Melissa means when she says I carry Ed with me. I am certain, in this moment, that he is a tangible part of who I am — not a limb or other body part you could grab and hold onto, but a part of my soul — and that's how I realize I have found Ed.

I can't believe it has taken me so long to see because it is, in fact, so simple. Ed is everywhere I am. He is in my head. He is in my heart. He is in my dreams. I realize this is what it means to be a soul mate. I realize he has indeed found me, and that I also have found him. Even though everything has changed, nothing has changed. Ed is right here.

My friends arrive for a potluck holiday supper and a Yankee Swap. Our swap is a riot. A candy dish has returned for the third consecutive year, this time accompanied by a tiny bar of sweet-smelling soap and a phallic neon candle that everyone suspects is really a vibrator. There are many jokes over that, each accompanied by a new ripple of laughter. Molly sits with us almost all night. She laughs with us, and I'm sure she can see that her mother is on her way back.

I clean up when everyone leaves, and I talk to Ed-On-The-Piano each time I breeze through the living room to gather glasses, wipe the coffee table, stuff wrapping paper in a trash bag. When I am done cleaning, I stand at the piano and sing to Ed. I place one hand on his urn and the other on his picture.

"You are my beautiful man."

I am smiling. Before I turn to climb the stairs, I say, "I'll see you upstairs, honey."

Jeanne and I sneak in a walk on Christmas Eve day. We start at her house and walk through a meadow, through the woods and into Look Park, where Santa's workshop is.

"I want to visit Santa," I tell her. "I want to sit on his lap and ask him to bring me Ed for Christmas. Who else but God has that much power?"

"Couldn't hurt, right?"

I am seriously thinking Santa is an option, but Jeanne is laughing.

Eli is more excited on Christmas morning that his "Browther," Darrian, Tommy's older son, is downstairs than he is to find a large plastic slide in the living room. Sally and Molly remember that Santa always put narcissus bulbs in my stocking, and they are wonderful surprises. We have birthday cake with dinner because Tommy turns 27 today.

The day is thoroughly delightful, yet I go to bed crying. A part of me thought that Santa, or God, might really have brought Ed home.

I have friends over on New Year's Eve. Jeanne and Mary are talking about a young girl in the area who'd overdosed on cocaine. Jeanne is saying how this girl had described to her mother the way her heart raced and raced.

"Sounds like Ativan withdrawal," I say, using tongs to plop Chinese food on my plate.

"Oh Jan," Mary says, turning to me. "It's not always about you."

I have to fight an overwhelming urge to run upstairs to cry with Ed. Instead, I choke down spareribs and fried shrimp, and I smile as everyone talks.

Before the ball drops in Times Square, I am alone in the kitchen with Mary, and I ask her if she really thinks I'm that self-absorbed.

"Oh sweetie," she says. "Of course not. I think I should give up sarcasm for New Year's."

But I know that truth is often at the core of a joke. I stop talking about myself, my grief, so I have too many words in my heart when I next go to Melissa. We chat a bit about some new furniture in her office, and then she asks me, "How are you doing?" And just like that, I start to cry. Hard.

"I miss Ed so much, and I feel like you're the only one I can complain to anymore. I think my friends are done with it, and I am just starting."

Melissa nods, gazing off out the window. "I remember after my mother died, after three months, I felt like I was just waking up," she tells me.

"Yes," I say. "That's how I feel, like I'm just waking up."

I realize then that that *is* how I feel. Without the constant haze of Ativan, I have woken up, and it is the knowing — the knowing that the nightmare I've had is not going away — that has brought on this new wave of anguish.

Melissa tells me she'd cried in the toothbrush aisle of a grocery store three months after her mother died because the toothbrush she'd reached for looked like her mother's; she says that up until that moment she'd been having a good day.

"You have one foot in Ed," she says. "One foot in your loss, in missing Ed, in the knowledge that his body is gone and you can't hold him, and you have one foot in the real world. With that one foot, you're building a business. You're being a mother. You're taking care of Eli. You're teaching seniors to write.

"It's a dance," she says. "And you're dancing."

I ask Melissa if finding Ed in my own body is real, if hearing him speak to me — if it is all really happening.

"Yes," she says right away, firmly. But then she thinks about it and answers more carefully.

"I don't know," she says. "I don't know if there's a Heaven. What do I know? You have to listen closely to your own experience. I think that's very important."

I gave myself a Christmas present — the movie "The Time Traveler's Wife." It has inspired me to travel back in time to warn Ed that he shouldn't smoke cigarettes. I picture Ed as he appeared in a photo taken in his early 20s. He is in Colorado, with a mountain range behind him. I am out of breath because I've had to climb to find him.

As I walk into the clearing, Ed has his back turned to me, his curly hair captured in a ponytail. I call his name, and he turns, and the scene looks like a photo on the wall — young Ed, with mountains behind him.

He does not know me. He won't meet me until he's 48.

"My name is Janice," I say.

Ed smiles, but looks puzzled.

"Do I know you?" he asks.

I explain that he will meet me in the future, and I say it as if it is just that simple, rational. I do not tell him I am his second wife.

Politely, he asks me for proof. I tell him that I know his father is a teacher and that his best friends are named Bob and Kelly. I tell him I know he cut off the tip of his left index finger with a hatchet his father gave to him when he was a boy. I tell him I know that when he was 12, his grandfather took him hunting, and he killed a rabbit and told his grandfather he could never do that again.

Ed studies me. "How do you know this?" he asks. He is no longer smiling.

"I know you. In the future. Please, I just need to tell you something."

He stares, but I can tell he doesn't think I am crazy or dangerous. I have his attention.

"Don't smoke," I say. "Please quit smoking."

"I love smoking," he says.

"I know. I know that, Ed."

I am studying his face, so young, so beautiful. I want to touch his cheek. Tell him I love him, but I can't. He doesn't know me yet, and he is 23 years younger than I am.

"Please," I say. "Promise me you will quit smoking. Don't just cut down. Quit."

There is a pause. "Okay," he says. "I will."

And as I fall asleep, I think it is possible that I might find Ed tomorrow, and he will be healthy, because he is not a smoker.

Instead, in the morning, Ed is still dead, and I do not want to get out of bed. But something is different now. Judy has started working with me, and each day at 9 a.m., she sends me an email asking for a to-do list. That means I have to respond. And that means I have to get out of bed.

When I email Judy, I tell her I was time traveling last night. I am so glad she is there, providing an anchor in my drifting life.

Even though people keep telling me I was a good caregiver, I have trouble believing it. I insist on dwelling on the moments during Ed's illness when I was not patient with him. I am consumed with one particular memory.

I had received permission from the hospital to work at home, but finding the time to actually do it was difficult. Ed needed my attention almost 24-7.

One particular day, I was feeling intense internal pressure to get things done. I had settled in to start on some projects, but Ed needed me to get his medication and find his phone because its whereabouts was eluding him. Then he needed help getting comfortable on the sofa because everything hurt. His feet were red and swollen so he needed ice packs on them. The ice made him cold so he needed a blanket.

It was impossible for me to think, to read a single sentence without being interrupted. It was impossible to work.

I finally got Ed settled on the sofa, and I was in my adjacent office, only a half wall between us. I was working on a patient information card about a new gastroenterologist, writing the text. Ed was about to fall asleep, and I thought I might have some time to get a few sentences written.

"Janice," he called to me.

"Yes, honey."

"What are you working on?"

"A card for a new doctor, in Dr. Meyer's practice." Dr. Meyer had treated Ed when he was hospitalized for liver failure. I was sure he could picture the rack of informational cards that hung on the wall just to the left of the receptionist's window. "You know, the cards that have the doctor's picture and information on the front."

"Photo," he said. "The doctor's photo, not picture."

"Right," I said. Ed was particular about certain words.

It was quiet for a moment, and I started to read again about the doctor's education.

"Janice," Ed said.

"Yes, honey." I was annoyed. I needed to do this work so I could keep my job and we could keep our house. I wanted him to fall asleep, now.

"Can you take me for a ride in the car?"

"No, honey," I said emphatically. "We can't go for a ride. I'm not in my office, but I have to work. I have to work."

I may have said "I have to work" a third time. I don't know how many times I said it, but I know how much it hurts now. I want a do-over. I want to help Ed put his flip-flops on his swollen feet and walk him to the car and get him settled with his seatbelt on and then drive for hours; that is the task I should have completed that day. Instead, I wasted precious moments, and I let Ed down.

Ever since this memory has returned I have fixated on it. It makes me feel so inadequate; it is proof that I was not a good caregiver. The fact that Ed died is further proof. I must not be very capable, right, if he is dead?

This is why I don't see the point in trying to be useful around my home. This is why I can't clean my house by myself or change my own lightbulbs or wash my own car or prune my own hedges or buy a new dishwasher. My dishwasher still does not work, and I don't know how to buy another one, because I could not save Ed.

Running helps me forget and because it naturally increases my heart rate, it also helps me to ignore the constant, rapid beat I have developed.

One night, I tell Molly I am going running, and as I run I pray. I say the Lord's Prayer, and I don't get distracted as I do so. I pray for Ed, and for my sweet little big brother who died when he was 10 years old. I pray for Peg, for my parents, for my children and Ed's. I pray for Emmett and Eli and Kisha and the new baby, Geneva Michael Godleski.

I say prayers of gratitude. I thank God for the fact that Molly and Sally are steady, competent. I thank God for giving Ed the way to find me. I thank God for allowing me to run. I do not get sidetracked in this litany of prayers. I am able to focus on them.

The next day, I go on a daylong retreat with leaders from the Episcopal Diocese.

As has become the norm for me, my hands and legs shake imperceptibly. We go around the room for a "personal check-in." The bishop asks everyone to talk about what they are least thankful for in the last year and what they are most thankful for. People talk about caring for ailing relatives, balancing multiple part-time jobs, family and spirituality.

And then it is my turn. I say, "I am least thankful for losing my husband." I pause. "And my job."

And then, without any warning, I am sobbing, hard. "I think we'd better skip me," I manage to say. I have lost my composure to the degree that I can't catch my breath, and I am shaking uncontrollably. Self-conscious, I stand to leave the room on unsteady feet.

"Oh my God," I say to myself as I find a seat in an adjacent conference room. "What did I just do?"

The rest of the day, I keep my emotions in control by focusing on a colleague's infant daughter; she is lying on a fleece blanket on the floor.

In the afternoon, baby Noel is cranky, so I lift her from a relieved mommy's arms, and we leave the room. We walk. We giggle. I find a chair in an empty room, and we sing "Pony boy," and she falls asleep in my arms. I close my eyes and say a prayer: "God, thank you for this new life. Thank you for the promise of another new day."

The bishop comes in and asks me if I want to rejoin the group.

"Isn't it great to talk to God with a baby in your arms?" he asks as I stand.

I am not surprised that he knows that's what I was doing.

After a winter snowstorm dumps five inches of snow on the ground, I tackle the job of shoveling our mammoth driveway.

The air is warm, and the rapidly melting snow hangs heavy on rooftops, trees and branches. The shovel scrapes the pavement with each new scoop, creating a rhythmic sound. I am working to its beat when my shovel uncovers a wrench mixed in with the snow. It says "Husky" on it, and it was made in China, so I know it is not a wrench Ed would have owned. It is not high-quality. It was not here before the storm.

I bend to pick it up and notice that it rests on the driveway in front of one of the rear tires of Ed's Jeep. This is the backdrop from my recent dream in which Ed helped me change a tire. This must be that wrench.

I hear Melissa telling me to pay attention to what I am experiencing. I am paying attention, so I take this as a sign that I didn't dream about Ed. I had a visit with him.

I have dinner with longtime friends whom I met through my first husband, and over dinner, they ask me if I regret leaving him, now that Ed is dead.

Regret?

"No," I say. "Absolutely not."

There is so much to say on that topic, such as that I learned that it's better to be alone than to be with someone you don't love.

Several weeks after Geneva Michael Godleski was born I go to visit. Geneva is beautiful, sleeping in a bassinet in the living room of the Beverly apartment. She has curls, and the same light brown, creamy skin that Emmett has. Kisha says she is an easy baby.

Emmett has gotten tall, and he is so glad to see me. I read him stories, and we play catch with a ball. He is still not sure what to make of the fact that his mommy won't let him touch what is in the bassinet.

The afternoon goes too quickly and soon it is getting late. I need to leave to drive to Judy's, where I am again staying over.

When I say goodbye to Emmett, he starts to cry: "I go with you." As I start down the stairs, I can hear him crying, and I know Ed would be pleased I have a connection with his grandson.

A woman from the Cancer Connection calls to tell me a bereavement group is forming. I say I want to be part of it.

I am 45 minutes late for my first meeting because I had trouble finding the building, and by the time I get there everyone has already introduced themselves and told their stories. Adrienne, the leader, says, "Janice, we've all had a chance to speak. Would you like to tell us about your loss?"

Eleven teary faces are staring at me, and as I start to speak, I begin to sob even though I had been feeling good all day. That the enormity of my grief is always tucked beneath the surface never ceases to surprise me. I tell these strangers that my husband died, that I lost my job, that I miss my husband so much. It is difficult to capture all of what I want to say into these two minutes. Two of the women reach for the Kleenex at the same time and pass the whole box to me. I know I am in good company.

Finally I am free to say what is on my mind, to be self-absorbed, insufferable. I am free to say that life sucks and that every morning I wonder how I will get through another day. When I am done, I ask the others to go around the room again and tell me about themselves.

There is a man whose wife was hit by a car while riding a motor scooter, a woman whose husband had a heart attack in their bathroom, a woman whose husband had Alzheimer's and died in a nursing home, and eight whose partners — and one whose twin brother — died of cancer. Hearing their stories is moving, heart-wrenching, yet also somehow calming, validating. In this room full of hand-me-down, mismatched sofas and afghans, I have found a place to bring my abject sorrow.

Several days later, on a Sunday, I am on my way to Mont Marie, a nursing home in Holyoke where Judy's mother, Bette, was taken following a recent hospitalization.

Judy calls on my cell phone to say that I shouldn't visit. Bette is not doing well. I keep driving, though, and find myself at the Barnes and Noble bookstore, the last bookstore I'd been in with Ed, weeks before he died. He was desperate for a magazine, but, presented with a wall full of them, didn't find a single one he liked. It occurs to me now that his telling me he wanted a magazine was just his way of getting me into the car; he knew I would go on a ride that had purpose.

I gather up novels and a few memoirs. I get books for Sally's birthday, too, and when my arms are full, I put the books down near a cashier and go upstairs. I don't want to go home. I wander into the health section and thumb through books, trying to find a reason for my rapid heartbeat and tremor, trying to find a cure.

In a book on healthy eating, I learn that the body's normal fight-or-flight response can flip into overdrive when a trauma is ongoing, releasing a toxin called cortisol. The cure, the book says, is protein and Vitamin B. On the way home I buy Vitamin B and chicken, vegetables and fruit. In two days, I am convinced I actually feel better.

I am like the bushes in my yard. Snow and ice crushed their lower branches all winter, pinning them to the ground, but when the snow melted, the branches slowly lifted.

We have made it through, the conifers and I.

Most eyes are dry this week in bereavement group. We talk about what to do with our loved one's clothing and belongings, and about celebrating anniversaries. There is much talk of memorials.

William is honoring his wife, Elizabeth, with a stone bench on the local bike path. Ruby had a potter make an urn for her twin brother's ashes. It is tall and lean, just like her brother was, she tells us, and it has willow branches that are entwined to symbolize their closeness.

A conversation begins about ashes. Some share that they were uncomfortable handling them, but Samir's story is amusing.

"I carry my portion of Jane's ashes with me in a satchel everywhere I go," Samir says. He explains that her family divided the ashes; he got one-ninth.

"When I go in a bar, I always have them with me, and I'm always tempted to pull them out and put them right on the table."

One Saturday, the married couple that cleans my house does not show up. There is grease on the stove and scum in the toilet and tufts of cat hair and dirt in the rugs, and I am anxious. Where are they? How will my house get clean? And then I get up off my office chair, and I get out a rag and the Murphy's Oil Soap, and, tentatively, I gently wipe the top of the piano, and Ed's urn and his photo. I wipe down surfaces and objects in the dining room and my office. I do the whole upstairs, and then I vacuum. I get down on my hands and knees and scrub the floor in my kitchen with ammonia and hot water. I watch the dirt disappear, and then I stand, and I look around my kitchen, clean and smelling of disinfectant.

"I did it," I say. "I did it."

It feels like a big deal, and I am in awe.

I am meeting with a new client in Three Rivers, a community with a large Polish population.

Walking me to the door, the client says, "Godleski. Is that a Polish name?"

I hesitate for only a moment, then recall how proud Ed was of his Polish heritage. Every now and again, after we'd made love, he would smile and tell me, "Janice, you're Polish by injection."

So, I look at this new client, and I say, "Yes. I'm Polish."

Ernie, in my bereavement group, lost his wife to breast cancer. I knew her in a six-degrees-of-separation kind of way. She was a physician in the Cooley Dickinson system, and when she died I made a sign to let patients know why the doors to her practice were closed.

Ernie makes me feel hopeful. His wife died 16 months ago, and he has removed his wedding ring and thought about dating. His body is not wracked with pain when he speaks.

"You make me feel like there's a future," I tell him in group one day.

Another member says, "Oh yeah. It does get better. I've had dates."

I can't imagine it, but I decide to believe them.

I visit my parents in Florida in February. They are renting a house in a dizzying complex called Indianwood, where the houses are small and all look exactly alike, arranged on streets that all look exactly alike, too.

Lying in the hot sun by the pool, listening to the splash of the water and everyday conversations about the weather and the heat, I feel the sadness and grief that has enveloped me for six months burning off my skin, evaporating.

I slather myself with sunblock every half hour. I shift from my stomach to my back, back to stomach. I am trying to even out my tan and my psyche at the same time. As my skin browns, something moves and shifts inside me, too. It is subtle. There is no moment I can point to and say, "That's when it happened." It just happens. I feel happy.

I am happy to be in the company of my parents. I am happy, too, because Molly is here with me. We lie in the sun, talk about college, read together while my parents watch "Judge Judy."

I find happiness, too, surprisingly, in the long ride home from Florida to Massachusetts. I take turns at the wheel, mostly with my mother. My father says he doesn't care to drive.

I am ready to be home, but content in the journey. I am not in a rush. I am in each moment.

In Georgia, the temperature drops to 54, and in North Carolina forsythia are in bloom. My father makes me pull over three times to top off the gas tank because the price is cheaper than it might be in Virginia, and my mother frowns and frets. After two months away from her home and her cat, she is in a rush.

In Maryland, the trees are bare but the temperature holds steady in the 50s, and that does not change through New Jersey, New York and Connecticut. It is 55 when we pull in my driveway. The sun is shining. Molly, who flew home ahead of me, is playing lacrosse at a field just a mile away, and I go there after seeing my parents off on the last leg of their trip to New Hampshire.

I pick up Eli at Sally's house and bring him with me to the lacrosse game. With other parents, I strike up conversations. I talk about the heat in Florida, the glorious heat.

I email Judy the next day: "I am happy."

I recognize myself. That's the best way to explain it. It feels so good.

I talk to Ed about it. "I'm not leaving you behind, honey. I'm still right here, and you will always be with me. I'm just choosing life."

In therapy with Melissa the next week, I tell her about the stretch of happiness.

"Why do you think you were able to find this joy?" she asks.

"I don't know," I tell her.

I find the answer on the way home as I am puzzling over it. Familiarity.

In those weeks with my parents, while my mother worked a crossword puzzle during the commercials of a reality TV show and my father, a diabetic, scooped ice cream into his mouth in the dark of the kitchen, thinking no one knew what he was doing, I felt the sense that the world was familiar.

In the hotel room that my parents and I shared off the highway in Virginia, the dinner and bedtime routines were routines long ago ingrained in me.

On this trip, in the company of those I hold most dear, I began to find my own core and feel the sense of home again.

On the six-month anniversary of Ed's death, March 14, 2011, I carry the basket of sympathy cards people sent after his death up to my bedroom. I have not looked at them since he died.

I settle under my covers, and start to read them. The first is from my cousin on my mother's side. I didn't remember that she had written. The next is from a woman at church, another widow who sent me a bookmark with a prayer on it. There is one from the physician recruiter at Cooley Dickinson. The next is from my neighbor down the street. "Thank you, Andree," I say.

I thank all of them as I open their messages. One card tells me that the person you love will always be with you. It's from Ana's grandma, who I have never met, but I know that because she is a widow we have an unspoken connection. After an hour, there are still cards in the basket, and I dump them out on the bed to see just how many are still there, and, my God, it is a substantial pile, an outpouring of kindness. I am overwhelmed.

The card that surprises me most is from my former neighbor, the one who told me at the bus stop that it was about time I left the Beacon Street neighborhood. His wife has written it, but she's signed his name. I think about redemption and forgiveness.

And I wish that Ed could see this basket of love.

In bereavement group, one Wednesday in June, it is Samir's turn to talk. He pulls his handkerchief out of his trouser pocket before he even attempts to speak. He is the only one who uses a handkerchief. He talks about missing Jane, yet another cancer victim, and he talks about staying in bed all day. He has roommates, and he says they tell him he must get up, but he refuses.

"I don't see the point anymore," he manages to say from behind the handkerchief.

"I don't know the point."

Others are crying as well. None of us knows the point, yet here we are, helping each other to find it again.

While I don't know the point yet, really, I have many moments when I do notice that things are moving in a forward motion. Judy has moved back to this part of the state and Beetle Press is alive and healthy, and I've bought myself a new dishwasher. I am coming unstuck.

I continue to teach my writing class for seniors at Mont Marie Health Care Center. I always bring a prompt to trigger memories and ideas, and today I have a bagful: an antique train, a tin full of mosquito powder, a candle shaped like an evergreen tree, a Hershey's cocoa tin, a satin clothes hanger, a teapot.

As I am getting out of my car, I notice Eli's leather baseball glove on the floor, and I stick it on the top of the bag.

Inside the nursing home I lay the items on tables. To my surprise, three women focus on the baseball glove. Sister Angela writes about how she's always loved baseball. Sister Mary writes about being a tomboy, loving the smell of her leather glove, and about falling out of a pine tree she'd climbed. And Jean, in a wheelchair with an oxygen tube running to her nose, writes about being a lefty ballplayer who had to take her glove off to throw.

I never would have pictured Jean sweaty in cut-off jeans, pulling the glove off her hand to throw the ball to the first baseman. But I can see it now. I can see her running, vibrant, breathing in great gulps of fresh air.

That's how things can go. There is grace when you least expect it.

I meet Dieter in my bereavement group. He is tall with close-cropped hair and square-framed black glasses and a goatee. Dieter's wife died last summer when she was hit by a car while riding her scooter. For the first few months I barely noticed Dieter. He didn't talk much, until one meeting when he weeps and talks about Greta for 15 minutes. He says she was an inspiration for his music. He says she believed in him. He says she was the best part of his life. He says she was his life.

In those moments, I think Dieter is my Ed. He plays guitar and writes songs. And he lives in a renovated barn, like Ed always dreamed about.

What intrigues me most, though, is that Dieter says he was married when he met Greta. That's what I think he says, anyway. When we have tea together several days later, at my invitation, I ask about this. He says he was already divorced when he met Greta, and he didn't have children, so I can't ask him the questions I'd wanted to ask, about how his children are handling the loss of a step-parent, as opposed to a parent. Instead, I notice Dieter's irresistible smile, and the freckle on his lip.

Dieter and I go out a second time for a drink. I have just come from seeing Molly off to her high school prom in a sea of teenagers in taffeta and silk and tuxedos, and I am giddy. Molly wore a short white satin dress, her hair done so elegantly, and she was laughing and smiling and beautiful.

Dieter is already having a beer at the bar when I arrive at the restaurant. I order a glass of Chardonnay.

We talk about Ed and Greta. I take out my digital camera to show Dieter pictures of Molly with her friends, but he is not all that interested. He has never met Molly, after all.

Then a tornado warning comes over the bar's television, and we agree it's time to head out so we can get home safely. We leave in a hurry.

When I get home, my power is out and my phone is dead. I take the photo of Ed from the piano and set it on the coffee table. I light a candle and pour another glass of Chardonnay, drinking alone for the first time in four and a half years, and worrying over that fact with every sip.

I start to cry. "Honey," I say. "He's not you."

It is so quiet. I hear the flicker of the candle flame.

"I really thought he was you, honey. I thought you came back."

And I cry some more, because this is just another night without Ed.

In group the next week, Dieter talks about the approaching anniversary of his wife's death. I talk, yet again, about the process of recovering my memories from Ed's last days. One of these memories was prompted by a recent trip to see my brother Jeff and his wife, Wendy. Wendy mentioned having a beach fire last summer when Ed and I visited them, and I am sure this means that Ed was inside sleeping while I enjoyed the fire with my family. That means I left him alone. I am thinking about this while Samir is talking. What he is saying applies to me.

He is describing how frail Jane was before she died, how she liked to go to parties but would only stay for a short time. He says he would take her home, put her to bed and then go back out. "Go back out." The words resonate for me.

I study him as he says this, and I notice he expresses no regret, no self-loathing or doubt or shame for having left her alone. It is just as simple as: And then I would go back out.

No one in the group is eyeing Samir as I am. They are thinking Samir did what he needed to do, and they are thinking that Jane was okay. Sleeping.

And I begin to think of the times I left Ed alone, and I think it was okay that I went running and left Ed asleep on the couch. It was okay that I returned Mary's casserole dish while Ed slept. It was okay that I sat by my brother's beach fire, laughing with my daughters and family.

I tell myself that Ed was safe, and he knew I loved him.

Judy comes with me to Molly's high school graduation. She is good company for me and for Sally and Eli, too.

The bleachers are packed, and we can't find four seats together. Judy and I find two spots on the highest tier. Sally and Eli end up sitting on folding chairs set up on the grass.

As if the seating arrangements are not unsettling enough, I cannot find Molly in the sea of blue caps and gowns on the football field.

I text Molly and ask her to stand up so I can see where she is.

"I can't, Mom," she replies.

I try to relax, just knowing she is, in fact, out there.

The chorus sings a song about the future, and suddenly, I am sobbing, wishing Ed was with me. It is not right that he is not here.

I cry on and off through the ceremony. Judy lets me be.

At home, with Molly headed off to a graduation party, Judy and I pour gin and tonics.

"Jude," I tell her. "I don't think I'd still be here if it wasn't for you."

I tell her about all the mornings that I forced myself out of bed because I knew she was at work and expected that I would be as well.

"That's part of why I came to work with you," she tells me. "I thought I could help you."

"But you hated your job," I say. "I thought I was helping you."

Now I'm really not so sure who was actually helping whom.

Chapter Twenty

Despite my Vitamin B intake, my rapid heartbeat and tremor are back with a vengeance. Some days the shaking is not so bad. Some days, it is terrible, and I have not been able to figure out a pattern. I have learned to live with the fact that sometimes I need to use two hands to drink my tea and that I have heart palpitations that suggest that I'm intensely anxious when I'm not.

I continue taking the Vitamin B even though it doesn't appear to be helping, and I do a 10-day detox program, but nothing helps. So I decide what I need to do is get stronger, and I meet with the personal trainer in my BNI group. I tell him I have a problem that causes me to shake and affects my balance and tell him I think I just need to get stronger.

In our first session, he asks me to place my feet hip distance apart, and he hands me weights to lift over my head. As I begin the exercise, he interrupts me.

"You're shaking," he says.

"I know," I say. "This is what I'm talking about."

"Can you make it stop?" he asks.

"No. No, I can't."

"You need to see a doctor," he tells me. "There is something wrong."

I make an appointment right away, and my doctor sees the same thing the trainer did.

"This is not Ativan withdrawal," she tells me. "This is something else."

She says I might have a neurological disease and refers me to a neurologist who can't see me for four weeks.

In the meantime, I visit my family in New Hampshire, and we celebrate my mother's 81st birthday in August out on my brothers' boat. As we're putting on sun-block, Al's wife, Jennifer, says to me, "Jan, you're so skinny. Are you losing weight?"

"Check your thyroid," my mother says before I can respond. This has been her advice each time I've complained about the shaking problem throughout this past year.

I call my doctor the next day, and she does a blood test. Two days later she calls to tell me I have Grave's disease, otherwise known as hyperthyroidism. She tells me to cancel the appointment with the neurologist and to see an endocrinologist instead. I manage to get an appointment in three weeks.

My problem has gotten so bad that at my BNI meetings my whole body shakes when I stand to do my one-minute presentations. When I tell a friend in BNI about my thyroid problem, she says she has noticed that my skirt always shakes while I'm standing; she thought I was nervous. Since I have just been elected president of the group, I can't have people thinking that.

So I call my doctor again and ask if there is any medication she can give me before I see the specialist on September 28. She says there isn't.

Sally, though, is a medical assistant and works for a doctor. And even though he isn't taking new patients, she gets me an appointment. Dr. Bigda prescribes some-thing called Propranolol. Judy is at my house when I take the first pill, and about 11 minutes later, as we are eating lunch, I notice the stillness of my heart and body. I interrupt our conversation and say, "Judy, oh my God, my heart is not racing." I hold up a hand. It is steady. I haven't felt this kind of calm within or had this kind of control over my body since last Thanksgiving. Dr. Bigda is my hero. He has told me that while these pills are only masking the problem, once my thyroid is removed, the result will be permanent.

When I finally see the endocrinologist he tells me the symptoms I've been experiencing since last Thanksgiving were all caused by my thyroid. He tells me my thyroid is the reason for other symptoms I've been experiencing too: fatigue, stomach problems, muscle weakness. He says my muscles have actually atrophied, that my eyes have swollen, but that I will regain my previous good health once the levels of thyroid hormone are regulated.

I email my mother to tell her the specialist told me that Ed's death — or the loss of my job, or both — triggered the onset of the disease. The endocrinologist said that's how it works. He also said I noticed it after I stopped taking the Ativan because the Ativan was masking the symptoms.

I realize that I didn't need the Ativan to dull my grief over losing Ed or my depression over being unemployed. I needed it because I was dealing with a medical problem, and the Ativan calmed the symptoms. I realize I was not weak as I traveled through my grief. I was actually very strong, toughing these symptoms out — shaking and struggling — for almost a year without any relief. I realize that, even though I can't have Ed back, or my job, I will once again feel good, and this gift is overwhelming to me.

September 6, 2011, marks what would have been my third wedding anniversary with Ed. It's also the date that his rapid decline began one year ago.

I mark the occasion by making a pilgrimage of sorts to the places we visited during his illness. I begin at an antique store in Northampton, where I intend to buy a ring with a gift certificate Ed gave me one Christmas. My intention is to then remove my wedding ring.

After trying on several rings, I realize I have a beautiful opal ring on my right hand that I could simply move to my left ring finger. I notice that when I remove my wedding rings, struggling to get them over the knuckle, there is no emotional reaction. If feels fine.

I put my wedding band and diamond ring onto the chain around my neck that also holds Ed's wedding ring. I like the new weight on my neck.

I pick out a pair of brass candlesticks and a deep blue vase instead of a ring. Later, I will light candles for Ed and put flowers in the vase, then lie on the couch and think about him.

Afterward, I head to the Poet's Seat Tower in Greenfield, where Ed asked me to marry him. I leave him a note in black Sharpie in the spot where he'd written his marriage proposal: "Ed, I still love you more every day. J"

My next stop is the Bridge of Flowers in Shelburne Falls, about 10 minutes away.

When I see the bench where Ed sat that day last year as I fetched the car, I square my body to it as if he is still sitting there.

"You were sitting right here," I tell him, out loud. "I knew. I knew what it meant. Did you know? Oh my God. Did you know, too?"

I walk across the bridge, the river below swollen from a storm the week before. I feel the breeze on my face, and I smell the flowers, and I feel that Ed is here with me.

Together, we take in each dahlia, each red rose, each vine.

It does not feel like a year has passed since Ed died. I can't decide how to mark the day. Since the boys and Molly are unavailable for a family gathering, I plan an evening with Sally and Eli and my friends, about 10 people in all.

We listen to Ed's music. We tell stories about him. We light candles on the gazebo, and then we eat Chinese food.

It's a fitting tribute for a beautiful man.

Several weeks later, after visiting Molly for Parents' Weekend at Plymouth State University, I drive to my brothers' restaurant and meet up with Jeff and Wendy. We sit there long enough, and drink long enough, that we need a ride home to their house a few miles away when the night is done. But the night isn't really done, because back at their house we drink some more. I haven't done this in years, and I feel the reckless abandon. We stay up until almost 3 a.m., and then Jeff shows me to my room.

It's the room Ed and I stayed in when he was so sick. After I've turned on the light I discover there is a wedding picture of Ed and me up on a shelf. I pull it down and put it next to my bed.

The Ed in this photo is the same one as my Ed-On-the-Piano at home, but something is different. So different. I stare at it, and then it hits me. In this version, you can see me. I am standing to Ed's right, my head leaning on his shoulder, my arm around him, his arm around me. And at that moment, I know what is left of us.

Me. Someone I lost long ago. Someone I never really knew, until I met Ed.

After a run on an especially beautiful October day I settle into a long bath.

The house is quiet, and I can see behind the closed blinds that the sun has set. I have work to do for a client, and I know it's time to get out of the tub. I pull the plug, and when the water has drained, I stand and hear a clink. Several clinks. I look down at my feet, and see that my wedding rings and Ed's ring have fallen off the chain around my neck.

I pick the rings up and hold them in my hand, feeling lucky they did not get swept down the drain, lucky that I noticed they'd fallen at all. It suddenly seems time to put them in a safe place.

I put them in a tiny ceramic bowl in the bathroom. I'm fascinated with how they have arranged themselves: My ring nests inside Ed's.

Epilogue

After I watched our wedding DVD shortly after Ed died, I put it in a safe place so I'd never lose it.

Then I forgot where that safe place was.

The next time I wanted to watch it, I searched the entire house — every drawer, every cupboard, every secret hiding place. When I didn't find it, there were many tears. I was angry with myself for losing something so precious.

One night, over a year later, I was having friends for dinner and decided to use my grandmother's silver. I opened the silver chest, and there, inside, was the wedding DVD.

I watched it again, then and there.

The first time I watched the DVD I had been focused on what Ed said to me. This time, I was struck by what I said to him.

I told Ed he taught me to be more accepting of others and more patient. I told him that, with our kids and him, I had everything I needed in the world.

Then I told him this:

I promise to always love you and to take good care of you and to be as good a caregiver and nurturer as you are, to anticipate your needs the way you anticipate mine.

Ed's gift to me was learning how to love and be loved. It was learning how to give and cherish and adore, and then give some more.

I am forever grateful for his divine renovation of my heart.

Acknowledgements

For the most part, it is the people who saved my life after Ed died who also helped me to tell our story. In particular, I am grateful for help and support from: Margaret, Jack, Riley and Lee Godleski and Sally and Molly Scaife for not only allowing me to tell this very personal story but for encouraging me as well and to Sally for being the first person to read the book and offer me feedback and encouragement; Jeff, Wendy, Allan and Jennifer Beetle, for believing I could do it and Harvey and Evelyn Beetle, for backing their belief up with dollars and lots of love; Eli DeJesus, for lifting my spirits in the lowest moments and being the most attentive, compassionate toddler I ever met; Bonni Alpert, for knowing a soul mate when she sees one and for being one herself; Judy Kelliher, for being the very best of friends, there in every critical moment and for always giving more than 100 percent; Mary Harrington and Casey Ravenhurst, for endless support, household repairs and for making Jell-o; Lisa Stowe, for being not only a great friend but also a fabulous designer and for developing the beautiful front jacket of the book and the template for the inside pages; Margot Cleary, for careful, thoughtful editing and a kind, gentle manner; Terra and David Missildine and Peter Duffy for compassionate feedback on early drafts; Craig Fear, for listening and encouraging; Jeanne Schubmehl, for many long walks and for her careful reading of early versions of the books, Deirdre Vinyard, for understanding what it's like, and to everyone else in our book group, for so much — from planning the fundraising party held shortly before Ed died to reading early versions of the book and inspiring me to keep going — Maria Bickar, Diane Monterosso, Ericka Prew, Jennie Southgate, Ali Childs and Joanie Daniels; Suzie Burgess, for repeatedly texting me and asking, "How is the book coming along"; Bette Kelliher and Molly Robinson, for sharing their own stories of widowhood and to Molly for calling me most every day to check in; Melissa Tefft, for endless listening and for teaching me how to grieve and how to be a stronger person in general; my bereavement group, for coming together like a family around grief; Steve Strimer and Off the Common Books, for answering all my questions about self-publishing at every twist and turn; and to the members of the Mill River BNI, a networking group to which I belong, for being the people who are going to help me get this book out in the world.

Note: Names used within this book are, in most cases, actual names. Some names have been changed.

About the Author

Janice Beetle is a long-time writer and editor for various publications in the Western Massachusetts area. The owner of Beetle Press, she also helps business owners and organization leaders develop written messages that communicate who they are and what they do, and she helps them to tell their success stories. She has published in newspapers, magazines — including Nick Jr. magazine — and journals. She lives in Easthampton, Mass., and this is her first book. Find Janice at janicebeetle.com and on Facebook at Janice Beetle Author.